On Gifted Elders

Awareness, Aspirations, Advocacy

Joy L. Navan, Ph.D.

On Gifted Elders

Edited by: Sarah Wilson
Interior design: The Printed Page
Cover design: Julee Hutchison

Published by
Gifted Unlimited, LLC
12340 U.S. Highway 42, No. 453
Goshen, KY 40026-0966
www.giftedunlimitedllc.com

ISBN: 978-1-7337758-2-3

Printed and bound in the United States of America using partially recycled paper.

To my mentors, gifted elders all.

Janice A. Leroux
Annemarie Roeper
Evelyn Freeman Todd

Contents

Contents

A Blessing for Old Age

May the light of your soul mind you,
May all your worry and anxiousness
about becoming old be transfigured,
May you be given wisdom for the eye of your soul,
to see this beautiful time of harvesting.
May you have the commitment to harvest your life,
to heal what has hurt you, to allow it to come
closer to you and become one with you.
(O'Donohue, 1999, p. 242)

Foreword

If ever a quote described someone, Maya Angelou's "Nothing can dim the light that shines from within" describes our author, Joy Navan. The first time I was profoundly touched by this amazing, inspiring woman was while reading her book *Nurturing the Gifted Female*. I was 49 years old and had been working with gifted children for 25 years, yet still hadn't acknowledged my own giftedness. In chapter after chapter I felt as if I were looking in a mirror. It was in her writing that I first experienced the concept of entelechy, "which connotes a drive in an individual to realize one's goals and achieve one's inner agenda…an imperative to fulfill her authentic self." I recognized this drive in myself, and it set me apart. I wanted so much to continue the legacy that Joy had started in nurturing our gifted females. I could not wait to work with Joy.

That opportunity presented itself when I was President of SENG (Supporting the Emotional Needs of the Gifted). In this book, *Gifted Elders: Awareness, Aspirations and Advocacy,* Joy writes about being questioned "Why don't you just retire?" During the period that I was President of SENG, I heard that question many times, but it was juxtaposed with my inner voice telling me, "I want to grow up to be Joy!" Once again, my life was profoundly changed by this amazing woman. Working with Joy on the Board of SENG, I was inspired to begin new goal-setting, questioning where I could serve the Gifted Community to the greatest capacity possible and continue to work with nurturing gifted females. It was during this time that I was also introduced to the concept of the needs of gifted elders.

Joy has continued to inspire and nurture my giftedness. I will be eternally grateful for the roadmap she has given me in my own pursuits to become self-aware, and to continue my own aspirations to serve and advocate for the gifted throughout my life. For the third time, my life has been shaken, stirred, and intensely moved by Joy. I was greatly honored when she asked me to write the foreword for her new book; never knowing that the reading of this book would provide me with healing, renewal, and a re-creating of myself. I was so excited to read the book, that I sped read the book the first time—just to see all that was there. The second time I read the book, I had to put it down repeatedly to self-reflect—to gain additional meaning through my own awareness. The third time, I realized that this would not be the last time I read through this amazing piece of work. Once again, Joy had provided me with a roadmap, not just for these times, but for the rest of my life.

One of the most beautiful concepts in this book is the concept of "the Mystery":

> [T]he construct of giftedness [which] bring moments of transcendence—moments in which we may glimpse or perhaps touch that which lies beyond ordinary awareness when we come to see ourselves as integral parts of the mystery—of the interconnectedness of the universe.

This harmonious composition provides an invitation to experience the ethereal feeling of true reverence.

The Be-Attitudes provided for gifted elders assists us in changing "goals to dispositions...perspectives that convey a sense of commitment to a way of being consistent and integral to who the individual is and how the individual chooses to be." These Be-Attitudes help us to move from existential dissonance to acceptance and renewal, moving us toward answers for "Who is my authentic self?" and "Is this the self I want to be in my elder years?"

For those of you who have not yet been blessed by meeting and working with Joy, one of the most exciting things about reading this book is that you will get to know her beautiful spirit through her writing. From "Blessing for Old Age" at the beginning until the "Celebration of Positives of Gifted Intensities" at the end, Joy's gentle spirituality, sagacious wisdom, and indomitable inspiration weaves through every page. This book is more than a collection of enlightened teachings, it is a call to action to pursue self-awareness, develop wise aspirations, and advocate not only for your own giftedness but for all the gifted elders in your life.

Blessings,
Lori Comallie-Caplan

Introduction

> *We did not hear the word gifted as a child. We thought we were odd. Even as we age, it is difficult to say aloud, "I am a gifted adult." We realize the differences in our reasoning, but mostly in our feelings. When loved ones hurt, we feel physical pain. A breath-taking sunset brings tears to our eyes. We lie awake at night, wishing we could set things right in the world. We labor to internalize the wisdom of Candide to tend our own garden; and, when we do so, it is with an intensity that could ignite the universe* (Navan, 2013).

Written a number of years ago at the beginning of my own elderhood, the words above awakened in me an interest in exploring what it means to be a gifted elder. Subsequently, several questions emerged. How does aging interact with giftedness? How does the interaction inform us regarding the needs of the aging gifted? What do common psychological constructs (e.g., efficacy, need for achievement) look like in gifted elders? What tasks of aging challenge gifted individuals? These questions and others gave birth to this book.

Historically, those who work in the field of giftedness focused on the gifted child and adolescent. Work in the field of gifted studies consisted of learning and supporting the intellectual, emotional, and social traits of our gifted students. Not until recently did advocates begin to consider and write about the characteristics and needs of the gifted adult. Currently, we see interest growing regarding the needs of aging gifted individuals, specifically, how do gifted aging individuals differ from others on the spectrum of neurodiversity, the range of cognitive functions and related behavioral characteristics?

The numerous responses I received to the quote above became an impetus to my own reflections regarding the many gifted adults and gifted elders I have known and who have touched my journey so deeply. One of my mentors, Annemarie Roeper, in her book *Beyond Old Age*, wrote of her experience as an aging gifted adult.

> Much has been said and written and researched about gifted children. Gifted adolescents also have a place in the consciousness of researchers. But it seems that there is a dearth of information when it comes to the gifted adult and giftedness in

> old age has not, as yet, caught our attention as a worthwhile subject of investigation. All elders have the task of keeping their minds carefully trained, and to keep on using them (Roeper, 2011, p. 23).

Annemarie's words bring me to the reason and rationale for this book: to share with readers and the entire gifted community the voices of our gifted elders, together with the current thoughts and research regarding gifted elders. These chapters bring with them a hope, a wish, and a dream. First, I hope that we may awaken an awareness of gifted elders' needs and create a spirit of advocacy on their behalf. Furthermore, I wish to inform family members and caregivers so that they may come to acknowledge and honor the giftedness of their elders. Finally, it is my dream to inspire all who interact daily with our elders to understand that, just as gifted students need differentiated learning experiences that respond to their unique needs, our society needs responsive communities and residences that respond to the intensities and wisdom of our gifted elders.

The Journey

In the following chapters we will journey into a world rich with the fulfilling lives and personal stories of remarkable individuals. We will gain insight into what it means to be a gifted elder. We will read of their continued aspirations in their seventh and eighth decades, and beyond. In understanding their nature and needs, readers will learn how to advocate for our gifted elders, articulating ways in which society can enrich their living environments and promote their continued productivity.

Awareness

The first chapter begins with a personal journey to situate the reader in time and place. The reader will come to understand the perspective and expertise that the author brings to the present efforts and some of the formative influences of present-day elders. In Chapter Two, after a brief review of the literature as it pertains to gifted children and adults, we explore the characteristics of gifted individuals in their later years. Chapter Three introduces the *Council of Elders*—the gifted seniors who shared their stories with me as a part of the research. Chapter Four presents the conundrum in which many individuals find themselves, namely, "When is enough, enough?" In other words, one of the primary facets of giftedness is the impetus for creative productivity, and many gifted individuals enter their seventies and eighties with an internalized need to continue producing and creating. However, in part due to societal pressures to slow down, to *take it easy*, and because of the realities of the aging process, which brings a slowing of our minds and a lessening of energy, we also must renegotiate the construct of efficacy—our belief in our ability to accomplish our goals. Thus, the subject of Chapter Five is that of efficacy, lost and found.

Aspirations

In Chapter Six, we examine the differences in "bucket lists" between gifted elders and other aging individuals. Just as giftedness is a qualitative difference in our thinking and our emotions in childhood and adulthood, it holds true in the activities in which we choose to engage in our remaining years. In a similar vein, we address the process of goal setting and life tasks in the later years.

Aging can be a depressing process for many. In fact, the incidence of depression in the elderly is prevalent in those with cognitive impairment, disabilities, or medical illness, all common factors as we age (Reynolds, Alexopoulos, Katz, & Lebowitz, 2001). For gifted individuals—with their heightened awareness and sensitivities—the loss of freedom, the confrontation with *never-agains,* and the physical limitations of old age may contribute to depressive feelings, even to clinical depression. In response, Chapter Seven presents the "BE-attitudes" of gifted elders, offering ways that we can face the realities of aging in healthy ways with a renewed sense of wonder and enjoyment.

Advocacy

In the last section, Chapter Eight examines methods that society can employ to nurture gifted elders through the creation of differentiated and responsive environments that address their continuing needs as gifted individuals.

Part One:
Awareness

Chapter One

A Personal Journey

Who we are is as important as what we publish.
~Paul Brian Campbell, SJ, Loyola Press

I ask that the reader indulge me as I share a little about myself as a gifted elder. It is not that I find my trek unique, rather my path reflects the similar paths of many elders in our time who have lived through the decades since the mid-20th century. Many gifted elders are children of the 1940s and '50s, as I am. We have witnessed extraordinary change in our society, transformed from a land of regions, cities, and neighborhoods into a global, interconnected community. Thus, in a sense, we, the elders, are the keepers of the memories and guardians of the voices that provide the narrative of an astonishing social transformation. Only through a thoughtful familiarity with our past can we discern the meaning of our present and glimpse our future.

My story began as the third child of four siblings and the only daughter of two World War II era Southerners, transplanted to the nation's capital in search of a way to provide for their family. I spent my early years in the suburbs of Washington, D.C., and later in southern Maryland, on the Patuxent River. Spending summers on the Atlantic coast, the Chesapeake Bay, or the Patuxent, imprinted in me a love of water and I lived most of the rest of my seven decades a half hour or less from either the east or west coast. Eventually, I came to view the St. Lawrence River as the fourth coast. She is my touchstone and my muse from which I presently draw my inspiration.

Renowned psychologist Alfred Adler proposed a theory regarding early recollections, which stipulated that early memories serve as a key to understanding one's beliefs regarding the world, what the individual finds meaningful, and the true nature of the individual (Clark, 2013). In other research, I used the technique of asking gifted females to share their earliest memories of being bright and found Adler's work to be quite helpful in gaining insight into their worldview. As an example of the projective faithfulness of early recollections, I remember one of the subjects in my book who consistently used precise and elegant language. When asked what memory reflected her early realization of her intelligence, she remembered her teacher's astonishment when she wrote the word *stag* ("because it had horns") instead of *deer* below the picture of a deer on a primary level spelling test. Even more remarkable is the fact that English was her second language (Navan, 2009).

My earliest memory of being bright is the recollection of when my kindergarten teacher gave me responsibilities that were more advanced than those asked of others in our grade. During a visit to my home, she told my mother that she expected much from me. Through the years, others shared their belief in my abilities, but it was much too early for the *G word*, gifted, to be voiced. Giftedness was not a construct used in our educational system in the fifties and sixties. However, I remember that, as a late elementary student, around the time of Russia's Sputnik success, my teachers selected me as one of a small group of students who went to a separate classroom once a week to work on "special projects." As a result of ability tests in high school, my teachers placed me in special classes in English and social studies and I was selected to be part of our high school's delegation to a Model United Nations conference. Looking back, I realize that teachers at both my elementary school in Maryland and my high school in California designated students with high potential for placement in enrichment classes and special programming.

It remains for another chapter to explain why my confidence in my abilities was never quite as strong as the beliefs of educators. Suffice it to share here that my research and that of many researchers in the field of gifted females underscores the vital need for the development of girls' and young women's authentic voice to avoid its potential loss. Bright, capable girls reach a point where their voices are silenced—either by themselves or because of the actions of others.

Eminent researchers in the field of women's studies, Carolyn Gilligan and Jean Baker Miller shared insights in this regard from their research regarding the psychological development of women. They reported that girls, because of the very relationships that nurture them, are in danger of withdrawing into silence when they feel that speaking their mind risks the loss of those relationships (Gilligan, 1982; Miller, 1986). Some readers, both male and female, may just now be growing awareness of their own gifted voice which was silenced decades ago.

How many times have we witnessed bright young girls who, in an effort to preserve friendships, go along with the opinions and wishes of their less capable peers despite their own beliefs, which remain silenced? In the observations of Gilligan and Miller, the silencing of self-expression tended to occur in late childhood or early adolescence. In my own research and professional life, I find that the quieting or muting of girls' self-expression, which used to occur in the early teen years, now may appear with gifted females as young as seven or eight years of age. In the same vein, boys may hide their intelligence rather than risk nicknames like "nerd" or "geek."

My personal journey is one of losing and finding my personal voice multiple times over the course of my life. As an adolescent, like many high-functioning girls, I went "underground" with my true words to fit into a social world that refused to celebrate individualism. As a college student, it was not until professors in my major course of study recognized and encouraged my work that I began to connect with my authentic voice and exuberantly recognized my ability to be a constructor of knowledge, rather than a mere consumer of the knowledge of others.

As a public classroom teacher in my twenties, thirties, and forties, I understood that one was expected not to stand out intellectually, lest others feel threatened. A transformative moment came when I completed my doctoral work and moved into the academic world. What a pleasure to be heard and accepted by colleagues eager to involve me in research and decision-making! With retirement, I became a student again in a clinical psychology program, an entirely new paradigm for me. I found myself once more at the beginning of a learning curve, and I was humbled by young graduate students, steeped in the literature and familiar with scientific research methods that I found so challenging.

Retired, I found myself at odds once again with a society that conveys the message that at my stage of life, I should not be concerned with creating a new profession for myself. More than once I heard the question, *Can't you just retire*? Yet, how wonderful to hear my voice reappear, strong and capable, as I worked with clients in clinical practicum experiences. Carolyn Heilbrun (1997) wrote of her sixties as a *gift of time*. Like her, I find my seventies to be an entry into new opportunities. Nevertheless, it is difficult to accept, and each of us—as we enter the final elderhood—need to prepare for an ultimate loss of voice should we find we must turn our care over to others.

Please keep in mind that the preceding overview of my path represents the life of one individual gifted elder. It is not intended to be representative of others whose experiences are unique and integral to their own development, personality, and setting. Rather, I offer it as a retrospective that may help in understanding the perspective from which this book springs. In the third chapter we will meet the *Council of Elders,* composed of the participants whose voices in this book form the warp and weft of our fabric of understanding.

For all of us as we venture into the mysterious new land of elderhood, our early recollections provide a lens through which we view the approaching years. Is our lens one of struggling to name our giftedness, or is it one of claiming the intellectual, emotional, and spiritual genuineness of who we are as highly capable individuals? Likewise, can we voice our reality in our personal and social lives, or do we witness the diminishing of our authentic voice as we grow old in a society that celebrates youth and marginalizes age? Such are, among others, the existential choices of gifted elders.

Chapter Two

Mysteries of Giftedness: Hello, Old Friend

Perhaps it is a sense of the mystery of life, the mystery of the universe that surrounds us, and the mystery that is within us. It is within these vast unknowns that we try to establish our identities. We strive to carve out a place that is known, a place that we can manage, a place that is safe, a place that allows us to grow our unique Selves (Roeper, 2007, p. xvii).

My friend and mentor, Annemarie Roeper, and I sat in her living room one evening overlooking the East Bay scene below us and in the distance. She remarked as she looked down that she saw cars, buses, and the rapid transit trains arriving and leaving the station on a distant street below her hill-side home. She commented how the scene was filled with people, appearing and leaving our view, rooted in their busy world with no awareness beyond the here and now. Then she pointed to the distance, where we could see above the hubbub below. We gazed on the San Francisco Bay, the Golden Gate Bridge, and above these, a dark blue night sky. She pointed to the sky and she intimated that there was where the *mystery* lies for her—the beyond.

The mystery, as Annemarie explained it, is that which is outside our reality as we know it. It is the unknown that we sense exists and which we might one day attain. In this regard, she often spoke of the gifted children of the new millennium who she observed to be much more in touch with the *mystery* than those of previous generations. She frequently said they have a keen awareness of themselves and their origins in another dimension. She sensed the millennial gifted children perceive themselves as mere visitors here in this life, in the world as we know it, and she felt they possessed an understanding that they would someday return to a larger consciousness—the mystery. As she neared death, Annemarie expressed her belief that she was resolved to embrace what lay beyond: "When we are confronted with death, that final line, we have to truly integrate into our feeling and thinking that we *don't* know what happens next" (Roeper, 2011, p. 43).

Like Dr. Roeper, I concur that many gifted individuals with whom I interacted over the years possess a sense of the mystery—of that which is beyond our conscious awareness. Their intuitive hypersensitivity to phenomena is a trait that allows them to make connections in ways that less perceptive individuals do not achieve. We will examine this strength further, but first we need to appreciate some of the more common characteristics of gifted children and adults.

Characteristics of Gifted Children, Adults, and Elders

One of the first traits we notice about a young gifted child is the voracious appetite for learning that he or she displays. Often, parents and caregivers observe this rage to know when children become engrossed in learning everything possible about one specific interest or issue as, for instance, dinosaurs, books, puzzles, or Legos. Unlike many children, gifted children are able to sustain intense concentration in the topic of interest for long periods of time. They enjoy creating scenarios, setting up problems to solve with manipulatives, and they easily lose themselves in creative play.

In addition to intellectual characteristics of gifted children, we observe distinct social and emotional facets of their personalities. Heightened sensitivities are a hallmark of giftedness, revealed as strong empathy, a clear sense of justice, and a powerful imagination, among other traits. More resources about gifted individuals are in the Resources section at the end of the book.

Gifted individuals often demonstrate intensities which result in heightened awareness and experiences. The intensities (also known as overexcitabilities) are intellectual, emotional, imaginational, psychomotor, and sensual (Dabrowski, 2016). A gifted child, adolescent, adult, or elder may manifest one or more of the intensities. Furthermore, the intensities may wax and wane at different stages of development.

Intellectual Traits of Giftedness

- Hunger for learning
- Enjoys problem-solving
- Intense intellectual curiosity
- Quickly grasps meaning
- Concentrated immersion in certain topics
- Thinks abstractly at an earlier age
- Intuitive understanding or predictions
- Profound logical thinking

Emotional Aspects of Giftedness

- Highly sensitive
- Passionate about social causes
- Emotionally intense
- Powerful imagination
- Genuinely empathetic
- Strong sense of justice
- Socially naïve

Note: Gifted individual may possess some of these characteristics as observed by the author.

As gifted children progress into adolescence, often we find their hunger for learning transforms into a drive to find meaning, to achieve mastery, and to learn ways to express themselves in unique ways. We know through research that gifted individuals develop their senses of self, of agency, and of autonomy much earlier than others. For instance, more than one gifted child shared with me their abilities to affect society through their community service projects. As they progressed into their teen years, they continued to develop their leadership skills with more complex and impactful activities.

The gifted adolescent may enter a complex, reflective stage of thinking and knowing in early or mid-adolescence, a stage that many individuals do not manage to reach or do not achieve until adulthood. The gifted adolescent often asks the existential questions: *Who am I? Where did I come from? What will become of me?* Consequently, a continued strong commitment to ethics coupled with perfectionistic tendencies may lead the gifted to display what may be perceived as oppositional traits in adolescence (Silverman, 1993, p. 3).

Early adulthood for the gifted may be an exhilarating time of discovery, especially when the gifted individual—often for the first time—has the opportunity to interact with *like peers* either in the university or work environment. Stepping out of adolescence, developmental factors influence gifted young adults as they begin to formulate a mature sense of self, while at the same time continuing to develop the intellectual and emotional characteristics that define them as gifted individuals (e.g., a strong sense of justice and a passionate dedication to social causes).

In a study of gifted students in a college honors program, Lee Kem and I found that young adults are aware of their high abilities as evidenced in their critical thinking and creative endeavors. Rather than finding themselves fitting in with other college-aged young adults, they reported that they still encountered misunderstanding and isolation when others did not experience the same intensity and impetus toward self-actualization. In addition, their desire to be seen as a whole person, rather than merely academically gifted, led to feelings of isolation (Kem & Navan, 2006). Fiedler resonated our findings, writing,

> They would like to think that they can join in with other idealists in making a difference in the world. They would like to think that there is somewhere they belong—where their abilities will be valued and their minds challenged, where they will be accepted and appreciated, and where they will find kindred spirits and friends. (Fielder, 2015, p. 43)

Fiedler termed gifted young adults "seekers," and described them as searching for both external and internal goodness of fit. They endeavor to find a profession that responds to their unique abilities and passions, while at the same time they examine their inner world, striving to formulate a clear and authentic understanding of who they are as individuals. In addition to searching for belonging and a sense of personal identity, Fiedler denoted this stage of development in the gifted as marked by idealism, optimism, and exploration. The young gifted adult engages himself in finding and developing relationships and often will become active in social causes as an outlet for intense idealism (Fiedler, 2015).

Despite their keen reasoning abilities, gifted young adults may need to collaborate with a counselor who can assist them in addressing diverse social and emotional problems. As Paula Prober shared in her book, *Your Rainforest Mind,* "Because their intensity tends to overwhelm others, they are told to calm down or quiet down, or, as one of my clients put it, 'to shallow up.' They internalize the message that something is seriously wrong with them" (Prober, 2016, p. 18). If the individual is a survivor of abuse, a dysfunctional family, or other types of trauma, the heightened sensitivity that is a hallmark of giftedness can often compound the intensity of the problem in the mind of a bright and passionate adult. In addition, the socially concerned, compassionate individual may feel helpless given the enormity of the injustice in the world, or the state of the environment, or the suffering of the poor (Prober, 2016). Finding the professional who is wise concerning the psyche of the gifted individual and who has professional expertise can often mean the difference between healthy growth or existential depression in this population.

Perhaps one of the most eloquent descriptions of the Self of the gifted adult is the following piece by P. Susan Jackson in her article, "Gifted Adults, standing like curious children, before the great Mystery into which we were born…paraphrased from Einstein."

> In their innermost core—at their best—the gifted adult is a passionate, deeply curious, sensitive and intense person, with a vast appetite for learning, for profound experience, for deepest understanding, for creating anew, and for contributing and participating wholly in the world.
>
> Their extraordinary intellect, oceanic emotions, communicative capacities, social appetites, and reservoir of uncommon talent pulse with the need for right expression, right experience, and right contexts, to be able to live authentically, and with verve. (Jackson, 2017)

Jackson continued that despite being so richly endowed, many gifted adults lack the self-awareness and explicit knowledge of Self necessary to actualize their potential and reach full development of their creative capacities. According to Jackson, the inception of Self can be traced to the individual's early years as a child with strong will accompanied by an inner self-knowing. The task that often remains in adulthood is to "learn that we must befriend our physical SELF, through movement and regular exercise, as the embodied SELF is a healthier SELF" (Jackson, 2017).

Moving into later stages of adulthood, many gifted individuals are still unaware of their giftedness, manifested as a rage to know and learn, accompanied by an intense drive to achieve. Another quality of adult giftedness described by Lovecky, is *entelechy*, an "inner strength, and vital force directing life and growth to become all the self is capable of being" (Lovecky, 1986, p. 574). Likewise, Fiedler's voyagers demonstrate "intensity, complexity, and drive" as they follow their well-deliberated path (Fielder, 2015, p. 68).

The Mystery

For many of us, along with the characteristics and development of giftedness described thus far, the construct of giftedness may bring moments of transcendence—moments in which we may glimpse or perhaps touch that which lies beyond ordinary awareness when we come to see ourselves as integral parts of the *mystery*—of the interconnectedness of the universe. In such moments we experience a sense of timelessness and an ethereal feeling of entering or being invited into to another reality. We may feel awe or trepidation as we confront the other worldly quality of the moment, especially the first time we encounter it. Afterward, often we feel as if we have received a gift to be honored and treasured.

> *Gratitude bestows reverence, allowing us to encounter everyday epiphanies, those transcendent moments of awe that change forever how we experience life…and the world.*
>
> (Ban Breathnach, 1996, p. 2)

Through my years of interacting with extraordinary children, several of them (or their parents) shared personal experiences of transcendence with me. I recall one young boy whose parents told me of how they came upon him one day shortly after the loss of a grandparent with whom he had been very close. The parents described their child looking up and lost in conversation, giving the impression that he was speaking with his grandparent. The authenticity of his actions, his spontaneous and animated gestures, impressed them with the sense that they witnessed a transcendent exchange.

A young child began our interview by sharing with me that she talked with animals. She said that she connected with them and that she could see what they were feeling and communicating to her, stating that they responded to her in kind. Her parents confirmed that their daughter had an uncanny ability to interact with animals. Another child stunned her parents as a two-year-old with the description of a traumatic event from what seemed a past life. She divulged details about the country and culture where the event took place that she, as a toddler, could not have known. These were children who *touched the mystery.*

I have experienced many transcendent moments in my lifetime. For example, I remember a summer morning walk on a country road, with trees on one side while on the other was a meadow still damp with the early dew. I rounded a corner, looked far down the road in the distance, and suddenly I was filled with an overwhelming sense of connection to a universal expression of love. During my walk, I had been meditating on where my spirituality was leading me. My answer came in the transcendence I experienced looking down the road. In such moments, we touch the mystery.

Intuitive Abilities of Gifted Individuals

A phenomenon similar to the experiences of transcendent moments that we see often in gifted individuals is their keen intuition. Intuition is the ability to grasp a concept immediately without a focused cognitive process, seemingly instinctively. I remember one summer as a little girl, not yet in kindergarten, I was standing beside the house we lived in at the time. I turned on an outside faucet and felt the cool water from the hose running over my hand. When I looked up at the summer scene surrounding me, I wanted that moment to last forever and for the season to never end. In that instant, the realization flashed through my mind that this was summer, to be followed by fall, winter, spring, and then summer again. No one had taught me the seasons. In fact, I do not believe could have named them. It was just that I gained an intuitive sense of the world and its revolving nature.

Intuitive thinking springs from the ability of gifted individuals to think abstractly at a much earlier age than most children do. There is speculation that the prefrontal cortex of gifted children, where higher level abstract thinking occurs, develops earlier than that of other children. We do know that at later ages gifted brains show distinct differences due to their higher levels of functioning. For example, research demonstrated that mathematically gifted adolescent males showed enhanced right hemisphere processing and higher levels of communication between hemispheres, allowing integration of sensory, motor, and cognitive information between the cerebral cortex on each side of the brain (O'Boyle, 2005).

Abstract thinking is an important component in intuition. I have worked with gifted children who were demonstrating adult-level abstract thinking as early as two and three years old. One instance occurred when a precocious two-year-old noticed my wedding ring and asked, "Who married you?" I replied with my spouse's name, and she followed my statement with, "And where is your husband?" The toddler had abstracted from a physical object—a ring—two different concepts: marriage and husband.

Emotional Giftedness as the Heart of Giftedness

Returning to my friend Dr. Roeper, I hear her voice once again telling me that emotions are the "heart" of giftedness. When trying to understand gifted children, educators and researchers often focus on their strong cognitive abilities. However, it is precisely because of their superior cognition that they are aware of and react keenly to a large portion of stimuli in the environment, no matter how small the stimulus may be. Their well-defined senses include reading the emotions of others, while at the same time not quite understanding that their own emotions run so deep, with all their consequent sensitivity and intensity, and without realizing that others may not understand such heightened emotionality.

Precisely because of their emotional giftedness, understanding the Self of the individual is of vital importance. We must hear and acknowledge a gifted person's emotions. For gifted elders, emotions are just as important and profound. We cannot separate cognition from the emotional, and we must honor the integration of both as vital facets of the Self. Nevertheless, we know from research that the strong emotional components of gifted children and gifted adults often lead educators and mental health providers who do not understand giftedness to misdiagnose them.

Webb and colleagues noted that a lack of fit between the heightened intelligence and sensitivities in gifted adults, whether in their job, social, and familial environments, may lead to stress or other symptoms that can easily be misdiagnosed as behavior disorders (Webb, Amend, Webb, Goerss, Beljan, & Olenchak, 2005). The high energy and intensity that many gifted children display when engaged in a favorite intellectual activity can be interpreted as hyperactivity. Many gifted children are both "bright" and "quirky," which, when not understood, may lead to a misdiagnosis of autism spectrum disorder. The intellectual "rage to know," which displays itself as the need to immerse oneself in the subject of interest (e.g., dinosaurs, Legos), might be viewed an obsessive-compulsive behavior.

Aging gifted individuals are at risk also of being misdiagnosed with a disorder due to their intensity and heightened emotions. The avid reader who prefers solitude in order to engage in her favorite pastime is labelled antisocial. The elder who requests access to technology because he regularly corresponds with others throughout the world is told to be content with jigsaw puzzles.

Imagine introverted aging gifted elders often thrust into a residential living environment where residents are expected to socialize and participate in group crafts and other activities. To paraphrase an aging friend when she told me that her family was urging her to move into such a facility, "I have authored several books, I continue to be professionally productive. What will I do in such a place? Make potholders?" Often even those aging gifted with dementia have an awareness of the disconnect between who they are and where they are placed. A close friend who I have always thought of as highly articulate with a keen sense of humor is currently an Alzheimer's sufferer in a horrendous nursing home. When I visit her, she brightens and smiles, filling my heart with her quips. However, behind the smile, in the depth of her eyes, is the awareness of her dismal reality.

Hello Old Friend, You're Back Again

How do the mysteries of giftedness, the intellectual and emotional characteristics, the transcendent and the intuitive, find their expression in the elderly gifted? In what ways can gifted elders, their families, friends, and caregivers recognize and value the facets of giftedness that they bring with them on their journey? The answers to these questions form the agenda and goals of this book.

For many elders who are gifted, the world of giftedness may be new to them. Our aging elders may never have recognized all the qualities that the gifted community would identify as characteristics of giftedness, starting with their keen intellectual ability, their hunger for learning, their heightened sensitivities, and their intuitive problem-solving. They may have spent their lives believing that they were flawed because they were so different from the norm. They may be in residential long-term care facilities that offer little or no stimulation or opportunities for enrichment. In addition, family members may treat them as children, discounting their ability to think for themselves and participate in decisions regarding residential care, end-of-life decisions, and matters as simple as deciding what foods are healthy for them. As a consequence, the gifted individual feels disenfranchised in terms of her own abilities to self-regulate and marginalized from family, friends, and society in general.

I was recently chatting with a friend, a former academic colleague. We were talking of the many projects each of us has begun in our seventies. He is a runner and used a very appropriate metaphor, which might resonate with gifted individuals concerning their continued creative productivity and their feelings regarding a life as yet unfinished. He shared that he felt as if he were just approaching the "starting line of life."

My colleague's words resonated strongly with me not only in terms of my personal need to be continually engaged and self-renewing. They also reverberate in terms of the mystery, of intuitive thinking, and of emotional giftedness. In so many ways, along with gifted elderhood comes the realization that the phenomena of giftedness are never left behind. Rather, they constantly re-present themselves as old friends, back again. Thus, the task remains to present a view of the world of the gifted elder with a particular eye to ways that society can recognize their needs and assist their journey.

Working Definitions

Having explored the concept and characteristics of giftedness, we should define the terms *elders,* especially as it differs from *old,* and *gifted* with regard to the thoughts and perceptions offered in this book. I recall words I read recently written by former

President Jimmy Carter, who published his book *The Virtues of Aging* at the age of seventy-four. He wrote,

> So then, when are we old? The correct answer is that each of us is old when we "think" we are—when we accept an attitude of dormancy, dependence on others, a substantial limitation on our physical and mental activities, and restriction on the number of people with whom we interact. (Carter, 1998, p. 11)

While I agree that the term *old* may provoke thoughts of dependency, limitations, the loss of some mental acuity, and a narrowing of our participation in the social stream, the word *elder*, has a much different connotation. Throughout most of human history and continuing in some current societies, elders are the wise ones, the spirit guides, and the teachers of the young: those whose existence sustains the present and guarantees the future of a people. Expanding the word elders to the term *gifted elders* presents a new dynamic in which we recognize elders, the wise ones, in conjunction with all the characteristics (e.g., high intellect, intensities) we explored as gifted. Therefore, gifted elders defined are those older, highly intelligent individuals who demonstrate heightened sensitivities and are capable of continued creative productivity.

In the last century or two, our culture transformed from one in which elders were part of the extended family in which three or more generations lived and worked in close proximity to one another, into one where the old live predominantly alone or in some form of residential assisted living. Our gifted elders are relegated to a marginalized existence as well. Their voices are often neither heard nor desired.

Nonetheless, we must endeavor to give new breath to elder lives. To paraphrase the words of Jimmy Carter, it is incumbent upon our gifted elders to reject the forces that pressure them into dormancy. If they must depend on others at times, they can still strive not to lose their voices through surrendering to feelings of helplessness or powerlessness. When others talk *about,* rather than *to,* older people in their presence, it is imperative that older people interject their voice, diplomatically reminding others that they are cognizant of issues, that they have the ability to participate in decision-making, and that they deserve to be addressed directly and respected.

Our understanding of giftedness in elderhood must go beyond parenting, teaching, and counseling. The term used for the types of modifications that educators use in serving gifted students is *differentiation.* The best models of differentiation are those that meet the individual where she is, view her *strengths* and her *needs,* then provide educational services that serve her educational, social, and emotional strengths and needs. Likewise, it is incumbent on society to recognize that our gifted elders need differentiated services that address their individual needs. The vulnerabilities of giftedness continue to threaten our well-being throughout our lifetimes and require the support and interventions of sensitive and compassionate companions.

Chapter Three

The Elders

Aging is not lost youth but a new stage of opportunity and strength.

—Betty Friedan

We are truly gifted by the willingness of so many elders to share their stories. Many of those who shared are distinguished in the field of research on giftedness. All are facing their aging years as gifted individuals, yet their paths reveal a broad variety of life experiences, of awareness of their giftedness, and of future goals.

Reflecting on the traits of giftedness listed in Chapter Two, each participant presented the characteristics differently in varying degrees, though intense intellectual curiosity and delight in problem-solving are frequent traits among them. As a preview, Mindy displayed a hunger for learning as she pursued a doctoral degree at age fifty-six. Charles was the trouble-shooter who was most content at work or with his philanthropy when helping a team find the solutions and resources needed to complete a project. Ruth taught herself higher mathematics and collected hundreds of math books. All the participants demonstrated both keen logical thinking combined with superb intuitive abilities.

Emotional intensity was also quite apparent in our Council of Elders, who shared their heightened sensitivities, their strong sense of justice, and their passion for social causes. In the words of Amelia, "For me, it is my duty as a human on this earth to try to better the lives of those who cross my path, even if it is simply to offer a smile."

One might consider the fact that the group is overwhelmingly female as a limitation. Only a few males chose to take part in the project. Additionally, the group does not constitute a random research sample. Rather, I invited the participation of gifted elders from several groups of gifted professionals which I belong to, as well as other gifted elders I knew.

Qualitative Analysis

The narratives received from questionnaires, interviews, and tributes form the bones of this book. They were mined and analyzed using phenomenological qualitative analysis. Specifically, after receiving the narratives, I compiled them into a database. I read through the database and as a common phenomenon emerged (e.g., need for achievement), I tagged it with the name of the construct or theme that it represented. I then collected all examples of each tag into secondary databases (e.g., goal setting, self-efficacy). Subsequent to analysis, I wrote the story of these gifted elders, which I respectfully present to you, the reader.

The Council of Elders

The voices and the vibrancy of the elders who shared their stories with me, as well as those of other aging gifted individuals, resonate throughout the following pages. The gifted elders in the group were sixty and older. The ages given are their ages at the time they responded to my questionnaire or interview. A few of my friends and colleagues had passed prior to beginning the research. Their stories need to be included and thus referenced to their tributes.

Carla (60)

Carla shared that she was "cast out" of her home as a teen and young adult and that she had to make her own way in the world. Escaping to California, she began a creative path as a writer in the television industry and later in publishing. Along the way, she learned that she had the gift of helping others to narrate their life stories, leading to the creation of a publishing company that continues to support her. Over the years, she raised eight children and, in addition, cared for several unofficially "adopted" children; created an organic farm and healing center; married and divorced; and moved cross-country several times.

Carla views her diverse journey and past trauma as preparation for helping others in healing ways. Her goals are to continue as a literary midwife, helping others develop their own literary paths, particularly helping younger women develop their self-expression. She serves as support for a parent, children, and grandchildren as needed, and as a community advocate.

Cecilia (66)

Cecilia began her undergraduate studies with the intention of studying music education and later changed to elementary education. She continued her studies, receiving a master's degree and then a certification in gifted education. She taught gifted students for 26 years and worked as a leader in her state gifted organization, eventually serving two terms on the board of a national gifted advocacy association. In terms of her personal music talents, she has performed for many years with a choral group, taking private voice lessons for the past nine years.

Cecilia worked full-time until age 65 and then began teaching online. She continues her involvement in gifted education, presenting at conferences, networking with others in the community, and subbing in gifted classrooms. She also volunteers at her city's performing arts center and her church, teaches elementary level enrichment courses, and assists her children and her parents.

Cecilia continues to be a lifelong learner as she and her husband travel with Road Scholars. She plans to continue traveling and learning as long as she can and to remain independent.

Charles (90)

Charles was a child of the 1930s. In our interview, Charles spoke of having four separate lives or life phases. His first three phases took place between childhood and age fifty-five. At ninety, he was completing a fourth.

In the first phase, childhood, he told of learning his most important life lessons. Growing up during the Great Depression taught him to distinguish between needs and wants. Beyond essential needs, Charles found that if he had any wants, it was up to him to work out a way to get them. If he wanted them enough, he had to work hard to earn the money.

Another valuable part of his learning during childhood was developing the ability to communicate with others. Because of his various jobs, he spent more than the usual amount of time during his youth interacting with adults. He believed that experience in the adult world served him well as he matured.

Charles reported that he had great teachers in school, and he took strong academic courses. However, college was something that neither he nor his classmates felt was expected unless "one was a doctor's son or a lawyer's son."

Charles told of the second phase of his life, which began after graduating from high school in 1945. He served in World War II, and afterward started college classes through the G.I. Bill. When the Korean conflict began, he went back in the service, where he was an Army Ranger paratrooper. He quipped, "I jumped out of a perfectly good airplane over 300 times."

During the war, he received several commendations and finished as a First Lieutenant. After the war ended, he was encouraged by his superiors to continue as an officer. He had already passed over other officers in the "pecking order," and his superiors looked for him to continue moving up in the ranks. But for him, being an officer in peacetime meant essentially waiting around to advance. "I am a guy that needs to do something," Charles explained. He found he could not be a peacetime soldier.

Beginning the third phase of his life, he returned to his home state and completed his undergraduate degree in business. He met and married his wife. "Best thing that ever happened to me in my life." He spent his professional life as an industrial engineer, first for an international electronics corporation, then as part of a consulting consortium, and finally as head of his own consulting group.

Charles earned a strong reputation, with colleagues saying, "If you don't know how to do it, never done it before, give it to Charles, and let him get it done." After six years with the electronics firm in Bloomington, Charles advanced to corporate staff and was sent east as a trouble-shooter for a team tasked with building control panels for the lunar landing module. His boss sent him to "go straighten out" the project, which involved Charles' stellar skills of problem-solving, pulling teams together, listening to them, and facilitating the procurement of what they needed from diverse places in the world in order to complete the project successfully.

Charles continued with the company, spending four out of every five weeks traveling. When asked to go overseas to help manage the development of new plants in Europe and Japan, he realized that he was weary of being away from home so much. He then went to work for a consulting company, where he was tasked with training the company management to do "what they told everybody else to do, which was manage your people properly." After several successful years in that position, he ran his own consulting firm until age 55, when he retired.

Charles described his role during the fourth part of his life as that of community advocate. He was active in several community organizations: Boy Scouts, Big Brothers/Big Sisters, Red Cross, Rotary, CASA (Court Appointed Special Advocate), American Legion, and others. He co-founded his town's community development foundation. He and his wife were big supporters of the local university's athletic program, funding an academic center for athletes, located within the athletic complex, where student athletes had access to tutors, individual and group study areas, and computers.

Charles shared that, in addition to putting their financial resources into supporting athletes, they put their bodies there as well by attending as many events as they could. There were some games, Charles said, when there were only three people in the stands—he, his wife, and fellow fan.

Until his passing, other major projects included a grant to fund iPods for the music and memory initiative at a local rehabilitation and nursing home. Through the community foundation, he assisted in funding and bringing about the transformation of the community amphitheater into a performing arts pavilion.

Dale (80)

Dale served in the Navy and then attended university, eventually obtaining a doctorate. A professor for over 30 years, he was also active in private practice as a marriage and family therapist. A talented musician, he taught music early in his career and continued his devotion to music as an instrumentalist in a band late in life (Andrus, 2016, January 11).

David (81)

At his passing, David left a legacy of service and conservation. A college graduate, he was dairy farmer for more than 50 years. He served in leadership roles in a variety of community agricultural and planning associations. Before retiring, he transitioned his dairy farm to a grass-fed beef farm that eventually met organic standards. He was active as a conservationist and steward of the Earth. His devotion to the environment was displayed in his establishing bluebird trails spanning two states. A man of faith and a lifelong learner, he continually renewed himself through his music and his love of agriculture (*Burlington Free Press,* 2016).

Deidre (68)

Deidre expressed her belief that she had extraordinarily good fortune on her life path since she never had a job for which she was pre-trained. Rather, all her learning and preparation for work has been out of necessity, whether the work involved landscaping or designing museum exhibits or teaching. A friend once commented that she "did well for a self-confessed person with no goals." Deidre felt that perhaps she may have subconsciously had goals and just did not recognize them. Rather, she did not limit herself with a preconceived plan. She described herself as a free spirit, open to opportunities as they evolved.

She began teaching gifted students with no teacher education courses and no state certification. Deidre describes this as being hired to "be" the gifted program. She eventually obtained certification and remained in the position for over 30 years.

Along the way, Deidre began to collaborate with teachers from another district in developing a primary grade thinking skills curriculum. The development of the curriculum led to the opportunity for her to serve as an educational consultant, a position she thoroughly enjoyed.

Deidre stated that she would have continued teaching if circumstances had been different (i.e., contracts, pension plan, approaches to education). Since retirement Deidre continues to consult, albeit less often since the demand for one-day on-site in-service programs has diminished, but also because she feels "out of touch" with the current school technology. She continues to write and to work with her own graphic art business.

Diana (67)

At 67, Diana continued to work and served as the "backbone" nurse for a small adult health medical practice. Semi-retired, in her leisure time she and her husband enjoy their adult daughter, grandchildren, and travel. Her bucket list included more travel and continuing to deepen her faith. She served as a support to her family and is active in service to her church.

Evelyn (64)

Evelyn recounted that as a young child she "kept my parents and teachers on their toes with all my questions and explorations." Being part of an army family was an advantage to her, because the frequent moves presented new people, places, and new things to explore and learn.

A quick learner, Evelyn was a challenge for adults. Thus, in school she was given special projects and began teaching the class in fifth grade, while advancing to higher grade level classes. Although she progressed academically through school and college and obtained a bachelor's degree with success, she had the social challenge of not fitting in. However, she found that social difficulties lessened when she was the organizer of activities. Though she desired to pursue medicine, she recounted that since she "did not follow the protocol of the time, the next step in my career was blocked." She was not accepted to medical school.

The world of work highlighted Evelyn's differences even more. Often, the fact that she was so capable and performed her tasks so well tested peers and supervisors. Additionally, she sometimes chose to do tasks differently, which was interpreted as challenging the system. Over time, she learned to keep silent and tried to blend in.

While working full-time, Evelyn started a family, raised her two sons, and intermittently attended school for three additional degrees. She shared, "Yes, I thought I could do it all and do it perfectly." Her career consisted of working a variety of jobs in various fields, all focused on helping people be their best.

Evelyn related that the turning point came when she reviewed her journey and realized that her intelligence and creativity were the features that made her feel so different from the general population. That led to exploring the dynamics of the intelligent, creative mind and the characteristics intertwined with experiencing the world by thinking differently. "I went from missing-in-action as a multi-talent to expressing myself effectively and with exuberance."

Grace (65)

Graduating with a degree in history and having no idea of what profession to choose, Grace followed her husband into teaching. Over 40 years, she was a classroom teacher, a professor, and a gifted consultant. In addition, she earned her Ph.D. in curriculum and instruction. At the time of her participation in the study, she worked with twice-exceptional children.

Grace's lifestyle and perspective evolved since her sixtieth year and she perceives herself as more spiritual, calm, and "in the moment." A goal of hers as an older adult is to coach younger people to connect to their higher self and use their natural abilities to heal. She would also like to serve children in foster care.

Gwenda (61)

Gwenda achieved a Ph.D. in clinical psychology at 27 in Ohio. She then returned to the Philadelphia-area and worked as a treatment team leader and director of group therapy in a residential center. When her two sons were young, she transitioned to private practice to allow for "more flexibility as a mom." They were identified as gifted and thus she involved herself in gifted advocacy.

With her sons grown and as she contemplated aging, she realized that she had no remaining family and her husband's family relationships were limited as well. Although somewhat introverted, she continued to maintain friendships and considered them essential to her well-being. Another result of her sons' maturing and becoming independent was that she searched for additional ways to use her professional skills. She wrote a blog to advocate for gifted children's social and emotional needs and participated in volunteer work and other creative pursuits.

Despite the demands of health needs, "Overall, I am more accepting, forgiving, and easier on myself that I was when I was younger, willing to accept my limitations, less concerned about what others think, and less tolerant of situations that waste my time and energy."

Leigh (68)

Leigh wrote that she wanted to become a nurse. However, as a result of pressure from a domineering mother, became a teacher instead. Leigh's early professional years were ones of fits and starts, interrupted by relocations, stopping to have a family, and two divorces. She finally settled into a position in early childhood education for 22 years. During that time, she achieved certification of advanced study in technology education. Since retirement from early childhood education she taught Lego robotics at a center for the gifted. Additionally, she taught artbotics, art quilting, and Mindstorms robotics.

Leigh personified the multitalented gifted older adult. She shared that since her sixtieth year, she became a quilter and poet, actively participating in creative groups for both. Additionally, she continued to train in technology, participated in three singing groups, traveled, attended the symphony often, wrote two blogs, and earnestly studying her family's genealogy. She summed up this stage of her life with the words,

> *I am more content with less material wealth. I have much more self-esteem and notice when*

> *others value me less than I would. I learned throughout my life that when I was faced with obstacles, I could just find another outlet in a different direction. I don't waste time trying to convince others to see things my way.*

Leon (81)

At the time of his death Leon, my colleague and friend, was still highly active in community service. He was a lifelong educator and steward of his gifts in his community. He was a former captain in the U.S. Army, a highly gifted professor of education for 41 years, and a teacher for 10 years before that. He was a mentor to many at his university and inspired countless young reading teachers to excel in instilling a love of reading and language arts in their students.

Leon had an ingrained commitment to public service. He served at the local, state, national, and international levels in his service organization. After retirement, he actively participated in service projects in the community and served on the local hospital board as both a trustee and chair. He was awarded an honorary degree of Doctor of Public Service by a nationally recognized university (Andrus, 2016, January 9).

Linda (60)

Linda, a beautician, began her adult life with the dream of becoming a nurse. Because her parents could not afford for her to attend the two-year, accelerated nursing school where she was accepted, she began working in an office and supplemented her income as a short order cook in a "gentleman's club." After marriage she secured a position as an x-ray technician in a doctor's office, at a time when formal training was not needed to perform imaging procedures. From then on, Linda engaged in a constant stream of education, both continuing education courses and self-training. She learned billing procedures, management, and soon became the office manager for the entire doctor's office.

Eventually, she tired of healthcare, believing that the field had evolved to a point where billing and collections took primacy over patient care. She trained as a beautician in order to pay for college. She recently finished an associate degree in business administration and then enrolled in a four-year college where she studied non-profit leadership. Her dream? To create and manage an affordable, self-sustaining retirement community.

Margaret (62)

Margaret had a hard first 10 years of adulthood, struggling with a poor college fit, existential depression, marriage, widowhood, poor remarriage, and divorce. Since then she has enjoyed an excellent marriage, three adult children, grandchildren, and several careers. Her professional path included serving as a lawyer, teacher, political scientist, and mediator. In addition, she recently trained in climate leadership, and she worked with her husband in managing and living off the land on a tree farm in the Midwest.

Margaret tried retirement but "really can't stay home and can't resist urges to continue to make change in the world." Since 60, she reactivated her law degree and became trained as a mediator and parenting coordinator. "I'm perplexed because I'm feeling and looking like I think my mother did at 40, yet I'm 62 and receiving Social Security."

Pam (65)

Pam published her first book in her early sixties. Her professional life began as an elementary and then gifted resource teacher for nearly two decades. After achieving a degree in counseling, she first worked in a mental health agency and then moved into private practice with a focus on gifted adults and parenting the gifted.

Insofar as changes since her sixtieth year, Pam responded, "It just feels like a continuation of my life goals of living a meaningful, purposeful life. Making a difference on the planet."

Rebecca (69)

My friend and our child's first pediatrician, Rebecca was born in Ireland and grew up in Alaska. In addition to her private practice, she was extensively active in local, county, state, and federal organizations. She also shared her expertise in the community, lecturing on child psychology and the family. A member of the first county health council in her area, she chaired her county's community development program and was influential in creating the first area Head Start program.

Rita (66)

The oldest of three siblings, Rita took on much responsibility at the young age of 15, when her mother died. She fell into becoming a teacher, having wanted to become a marine biologist, but recognizing the impossibility for a woman in New Zealand during the 1960s. She taught for 21 years, finishing her B.Ed. degree while working full-time. She discovered a passion for gifted education, was the first in her country to start a Future Problem Solving program, and continued as national director of the organization and on two of its international committees. As a professional development advisor, she served over schools, providing development in science, English, technology education, gifted education, and the national curriculum.

"I was given the opportunity to complete my master's degree, but after getting an A+ on my first papers, I proved that I could do it [on my own] if I wanted. I don't learn by being told what to learn by someone else." She enjoyed online courses, MOOCs (massive open online courses), despite the difficulty of finding the time to complete them. As a result of her accomplishments, Rita received the Queen's Service Medal for her work in gifted education.

Ruth (80)

After graduating from college with a degree in mathematics in 1958, Ruth found that companies did not hire women mathematicians. "So teaching was the alternative, which I have never regretted for the 59 years that I have been teaching mathematics in one capacity or another." She viewed being a masterful teacher as an "art form and like most endeavors it must be practiced and honed."

When Ruth turned 70, she felt she needed a new goal in life, so she entered a Ph.D. program and finished at 75. "It was hard as hell, but I stayed in the struggle." Staying in the struggle is a fundamental concept she teaches her students about math and life.

Sandra (63)

Sandra began working in clerical jobs after high school, while at the same time attending night school. She completed an associate degree in business after 14 years. As she continued working, she earned a bachelor's in sociology with the goal of continuing in graduate school and completing a master's in social work. Due to life circumstances, she was unable to follow that course and achieved an alternative certificate in special education, eventually becoming a social studies teacher.

During her teaching career, she taught a variety of courses in the social sciences, such as world history, psychology, and sociology. She also taught at night, both in-person and online. She was additionally certified to teach English as a Second Language and in gifted education.

Sheila (62)

Sheila has a Master of Divinity degree with a focus on ethics and social justice. Her involvement in community work and social justice began as a community health organizer in Appalachia and continued as a hospital chaplain in Brooklyn and at a prestigious university in the Northeast. After the loss of a beloved brother to AIDS, she became the first HIV/AIDS health educator at the same university, followed by continued service in health education. She also served as director for community relations and associate director at the university health center.

Stephanie (61)

Stephanie grew up in a dysfunctional, addictive family with an overcritical mother. She earned a degree in education and followed with a diploma in special education and another in minimal brain dysfunction. A move from one continent to another as a single mother with two children "meant that I finally broke free of family and took sole responsibility for my children and my personal future."

As a special-needs coordinator, she recounted that she was fortunate to meet a very gifted student who awakened in her the desire to advocate for and support gifted children and their families. Her interest led her to complete two master's degrees in gifted education, the second finished after age 55. Since then, she continued to facilitate parent discussion groups, mentor gifted children, and provide extension and enrichment classes to children in the community.

Vivian (74)

Vivian is the mother of three profoundly gifted adult children. She worked professionally in non-profit and healthcare management. Her personal interests involved volunteering in education, performing arts, and fine arts. Her goals for future years were to stay well and active. Additionally, she hoped to maintain her independent living and continue to develop her lifelong interests and activities.

Will (71)

Will studied education and received a B.A. in education, followed by one M.A. in guidance and counseling and a second in educational administration. His final degree was a specialist degree in educational administration. During his professional career he was a middle school teacher, followed by a high school guidance counselor and assistant high school principal. He ended his professional career as the director of his district's family resource center.

Will received his state's Principal of the Year award. Additionally, he mentored 100 interns in educational administration. As a public servant he served as a city councilman for 20 years and as mayor for four. Furthermore, he served on several community service boards as member and officer and received several awards in that regard (Morris, 2012, February 3).

Emerging Elders

I chose to define and separate respondents between ages 55 and 60 because of the need to tell the stories of several who have accomplished so much prior to their elderhood. These emerging elders are poised for full entry into gifted elderhood as evidenced by their accomplishments, their need for continued growth, their resilience, their impetus to serve, and their multiple careers. Their voices are merged into these important constructs of success.

Continued Growth

In the years between 55 and 60, many people anticipate leaving their careers and moving into retirement. However, our participants who were moving toward gifted elderhood were contemplating continued productivity. In some cases, they were initiating new professional endeavors. For example, Alice, who was widowed at 54, surprised herself with the grace and strength with which she transitioned from a partnership to life on her own. She continued to grow and achieve.

Amelia presents another example of continued growth. Amelia spent her adult years teaching in public and private education and homeschooling. She now is a writer and advocate for the gifted. She stated what I observed in all of those moving toward elderhood, "I have finally gained the confidence and wisdom to approach life, not as something that happens to me, but as something I have control over, can change or choose to ignore."

As she approaches elderhood, Gracelyn also exhibits continued growth. After an active career in health administration, Gracelyn transitioned at age 55 into a new position that "engages all of my experience, bringing innovative solutions to the challenge of creating access to health services in rural and underserved areas." In addition, it satisfied the need she had to "engage in work related to social justice issues, behavioral health, and wholistic solutions."

Gracelyn also learned meditation and is now a meditation trainer. As she continued to deepen her spiritual connections, she asserted that the spiritual focus guided the work, the service, and the personal facets of her life.

Similarly, Lana, already with an abundance of degrees and certifications, declared, "I needed another area of challenge (after age 55) and added family law as an area of professional development." Likewise, Mindy has a master's in curriculum and taught 27 years, 14 of them as a teacher of the gifted. She raised two gifted sons and now continues to study, with the goal of earning an Ed.D.

Resilience and Drive

Sarah exemplified resilience and drive in emerging elders. She shared that her path had been somewhat circuitous. Growing up in New Zealand, she comes from "the last generation where girls were destined to be nurses, teachers, or secretaries for a few years before they married." Her father insisted that she move from the top academic stream in high school to the commercial track to prepare her to work in an office. Sarah reflected that school then became "soul-destroying," and as a result her academic achievement dropped to failing, apart from English and history. She left school at 15 and worked in routine clerical jobs. After two years she took correspondence courses to gain entrance to university to study teacher training. Once a teacher, she earned a B.A. in history after seven years of full-time teaching and part-time study. An insatiable learner, she continued her studies while rising to department head and dean of her school, while simultaneously studying for a postgraduate diploma in religious studies. When her children were born, she both worked part-time and earned a diploma in childbirth education, becoming a doula and childbirth educator. Despite all her diplomas, she shared, "If I need the piece of paper to achieve a goal, I will pursue what is needed; but otherwise I much prefer to direct my own learning path and I am still an avid learner." At the time of her participation in the study, Sarah was a leading and active advocate for gifted education in her country.

Vanessa's story was another example of resilience and drive. She finished high school and started college at age 16. She worked during the day and attended college at night completing her last degree, a master's in business administration, in her early thirties. She began working as a legal secretary at 17 and then worked for a municipality rising to the position of city auditor. She transitioned to a multi-state media conglomerate, after which she managed her own consulting business for 22 years. She has served on numerous boards, both locally and statewide, with her most recent position on an internationally renowned hospital board.

Impetus to Serve

Alice always felt a strong desire to contribute to the world. She took part in and initiated many service projects as a college student. Having lost a spouse, she shared that she is inspired to "cherish each moment," which entails cherishing and accepting Self, as well as striving to live a more authentic life.

Gracelyn, whom we met in "Continued Growth," also demonstrates an impetus to serve by sponsoring others in meditation pursuits, taking an active role in diverse recovery groups, working with women in a regional prison, and assisting in the coordination and training for a local emergency response team. Mindy, also from "Continued Growth," was an active volunteer for Ronald McDonald House, cared for an elderly parent, and was a year-long after-school tutor. Toni had an active teaching career and moved on to serve as a dynamic advocate for the gifted locally and statewide.

Susana, another illustration of service, served as the U.S. representative to a commission charged with setting global human resource management standards and was elected to lead the recruitment standard. She continues to lead as Vice Chair of the U.S. Committee for International Human Resources Standards. Recently, she was asked to be representative on the review board for the Talent Board, a leader in the recruitment industry. Susana was also selected as a board member for the Human Resource

Management Certification Institute (HRCI), certifying H.R. professionals around the world.

Multiple Careers

In the last few decades it has become increasingly common for individuals to experience multiple careers, either sequentially or concurrently. For our gifted elders and those gifted individuals approaching elderhood, the practice of moving from one profession already existed. Consider Hannah, a member of our approaching elderhood cohort. Hannah finished first in her class at law school and began her career as clerk for the chief judge of a circuit court for the United States Court of Appeals. She also worked for a labor-supporting law firm, a large corporate firm, and in private practice as a pro bono advocate for first amendment work. After her first child was born, she left private practice for a better balance, when she worked for the National Endowment for the Arts and most recently for the Library of Congress.

Another illustration of multiple careers among the approaching elderhood cohort is Laura. After college Laura progressed directly into a doctoral program followed by three years of post-doc teaching and research. Subsequently, she began a tenure track position as a faculty member and attained a full professorship. She was increasingly asked to take on service and administrative roles as graduate director, undergraduate director, program officer for the National Science Foundation. Ultimately, she served as associate dean of her college.

We hear in their narratives that gifted individuals approaching elderhood are prepared for admission into the Council of Elders, given their accomplishments, need for continued growth, resilience, drive, and commitment to serve.

Chapter Four

Elusive Love Affair: Achievement from an Elder's Perspective

Science is like a love affair with nature; an elusive, tantalising mistress. It has all the turbulence, twists and turns of romantic love, but that's part of the game.

(Ramachandran in Nagaswami, 2016)

Need for achievement (N-Ach) is a psychological disposition that individuals have and which manifests itself as a drive or impetus towards accomplishment. As a psychological variable, some experience the need more intensely than others. In addition to their other intensities, we frequently identify gifted adults by their strong drive toward attaining difficult goals and their incentive to constantly be learning, creating, and improving themselves.

Achievement in the Gifted Elder

How does N-Ach and its outcome look in the gifted elder? In my own case, although N-Ach was ever present, its realization took a circuitous route. A late-bloomer, I completed a B.A. and M.A., then took time off from my studies to care for our children while teaching full-time. Achieving a Ph.D. in my early fifties, I retired from high school teaching and entered academia. Retiring for a second time after 16 years at university, I promptly returned to life as a student, completing a master's in clinical psychology at age 72. Currently I serve as a licensed psychological associate (LPA) and an educational consultant.

My story is not unique. I know and interviewed many elders whose professional paths took a convoluted path like mine. Additionally, most of the elders who have shared their stories with me continue to learn and remain productive into their later years. N-Ach is ever present and persistently driving them forward.

From our Council of Elders, Charles provides a prime example. He described four phases of his life, with his last three as periods of immense productivity. His military experience and professional life occurred prior to elderhood, and from age 55 through 90, he was richly productive as a community activist and philanthropist. Another is Linda, who is currently winding down her third career and completing a degree in non-profit leadership studies in order to expand her knowledge of how to start and sustain a non-profit. Her goal is to purchase land and create a vibrant retirement community for older adults, where they can remain active through gardening, use of a common maker space, continue their creative pursuits, and socialize through other activities.

In my observation, many gifted elders in our group of participants travel a similar path. They may have experienced two, three, or more professional phases and then found that in their older years they were not prepared to *hang up their spurs*. Rather, they opted to throw themselves into new initiatives, ventures tempered by variables such as health, needs of others, and differing levels of vitality.

Miles to Go Before We Sleep

Among the Council of Elders, achievement follows diverse pathways as well. In terms of advocacy and service, we observed David who, after a lifetime of working the land, immersed himself in environmental advocacy. Others like Dale and Diana followed their faith pathways, serving their church families. Cecilia was an active advocate for gifted children.

Advocacy and service are two themes that appeared often in our Council of Elders. For example, Carla became a literary midwife, assisting others in writing their story. In addition, she advocated in her community. Edith actively supported gifted individuals with mild or moderate brain injuries. Another model of service is Grace, who mentors a highly gifted immigrant. As a final exemplar, Gracelyn, in addition to serving as a leader in several health-related community service organizations, also serves as a mentor to women in recovery from addiction.

Another dominant theme in the area of achievement is that of lifelong learning. Among the many examples of formal and informal study and training in elderhood, we note that a substantial number of our Council of Elders saw retirement and aging as a door opening to new understandings and knowledge. Learning varied, with some pursuing independent learning, others college courses or degrees. Two participants had the goal of achieving doctoral degrees and one finished a Ph.D. at the age of 75.

Some members of the Council focused on learning new technology or acquired more skills in their area of expertise in order to continue working in their fields. Others found the joy of taking on new learning unrelated to their professional lives, learning beekeeping, photography, quilting, or other hobbies. One member mentioned learning through the Road Scholars organization and another Coursera. In all, remaining cognitively engaged was of considerable importance to our gifted elders.

When is Enough, Enough?

To continue growing, learning, and achieving is part of the nature of giftedness for many adults and elders. The *intellectual imperative* we might call it, or the impetus to self-actualize oneself—to fulfill the blueprint of potentiality we were born with. For some it is impossible to turn off the achievement switch. Consider Annemarie Roeper, who continued writing and publishing into her nineties. A few years before her death and continuing until her final months, she often shared with me her lament at the growing disparity and disconnection between her mind and her body.

The discrepancy between what we still want to achieve and the limited energy and concomitant health needs of elderhood emerges during our waning years in stark contrast to the exuberance and limitless zest we remember as recently as seemingly yesterday. The life needs of others often disrupted achievement plans of participants in the study. Women in particular placed their professional and creative plans on hold as they cared for aging parents. More discouraging are the reactions of some that divulge their belief that we should be happy to rest, take it easy, and enjoy our golden years of leisure. Yet, to paraphrase the poet, we have promises to keep. I think of Margaret, 62, who recently retired. In the last few years, in addition to working alongside her husband in maintaining a tree farm, she reactivated her law degree and trained as a mediator, and now works in the court system. Additionally, she trained and is now active as a climate reality leadership corps member.

A Transformative View of Achievement

It is essential that we recognize the qualitative difference we see in N-Ach insofar as gifted individuals are concerned. Achievement need not be an accumulation of awards or accolades, nor is it talent development. Rather, achievement is the personal development of one's unique Self, with all its cognitive strengths, strong intensities, and meta-awareness (Tolan & Piechowski, 2013).

If we view achievement as a component of gifted characteristics (e.g., intense intellectual curiosity, passion for social causes, strong sense of justice), perhaps another perspective of achievement is appropriate. In gifted elders who continue to feel an intense impetus to continue to learn and to serve, what we may be observing is N-Ach transformed into self-actualization. Achievement for the sake of achievement is no longer viable as a construct when the individual transforms N-Ach into a drive to fulfill a mission, to solve an ethical or social problem, or to contribute to a more equitable society.

Self-actualization is a psychological construct proposed by Abraham Maslow as the highest level of his Hierarchy of Needs (Maslow, 1968). He defined self-actualization as "the desire for self-fulfillment, namely tendency for him to become actualized in what he is potentially" (Maslow, 1943, p. 383). Kaufman revisited Maslow's work and conducted research with findings that indicate self-actualization as a vital construct continues to be relevant to our understanding motivation and psychological well-being. Moreover, in his research Maslow's characteristics of a self-actualizing individual remain vibrant in our 21st century (Kaufman, 2018).

Characteristics of self-actualization that are prominent in the narratives of our emerging elders and Council of Elders include acceptance, authenticity, purpose, humanitarianism, peak experiences, and creative spirit (Kaufman, 2018). For example, Charles and several others chose to enact their sense of purpose in dedicating their waning years in service to community. Evelyn personified authenticity in her refusal to "play the game," albeit at the expense of entry into medical school. Several elders in our group maintained or took up new creative interests after retirement.

Life Tasks

Self-actualizing elders who continue to be propelled forward by N-Ach, which is our drive to continue to contribute to our world, must master a few tasks. First, we must negotiate a truce between our minds and our bodies. We should be ever mindful of when our energy is strong and take advantage of those times to work.

Another task is to recognize that our time is not limitless and to decide what we can and what we will not accomplish during our final years. I recently had to bow out of a project with a group of colleagues whom I love and respect because it was clear that I could not participate with them, finish my clinical psychology studies, prepare for the licensure exam, and have the energy left for my writing agenda.

A third task for the achievement-oriented elder is to reconcile oneself with the fact that enough *is* enough. In other words, what we have accomplished, if it contributed to the betterment of our loved ones, our profession, and our world, is worthy. The elusive love affair is a success.

Chapter Five

Exercises in Efficacy

People's beliefs in their personal efficacy play a paramount role in how they organize, create, and manage the environment that affects their developmental pathways.

(Bandura, 1997, p. 163)

I shared in the previous chapter that at the age of 72 I defended a thesis in clinical psychology. A master's degree should seem like "old hat" for someone with my academic background. However, the journey through my most recent master's program was a harrowing process for several reasons. As with many elders, I dealt with health problems. But aside from those, I found myself on a constant roller coaster as I struggled to learn in what was an entirely new paradigm for someone schooled in the liberal arts. It was a journey of efficacy, lost and gained.

In our state, with the master's degree and successful completion of a national exam, one may practice as a licensed psychological associate under the supervision of a licensed clinical psychologist. A successful defense of my thesis was the last step in completing the degree, allowing me to turn my attention to preparing for the licensure exam.

Efficacy, Lost and Gained

Self-efficacy, a psychological construct, is a belief that one is capable of achieving success with a given task (Bandura, 1997). In *Nurturing the Gifted Female: A Guide for Educators and Parents* (Navan, 2009), I described different areas of self-efficacy. One area is intellectual efficacy, where the individual feels capable of mastering and applying knowledge. Emotional efficacy is in play when one perceives Self as capable of moderating emotional responses in order to ensure well-being. The third area, behavioral efficacy, is the self-belief that the individual has of the ability to act in a manner that is consistent with who she is.

In the *Nurturing the Gifted Female,* I described several gifted young women who possessed strong self-efficacy. Self-efficacy was realized in their perceptions of themselves as capable of setting challenging goals and having the ability to accomplish those goals. When I asked one of the girls what was the source of her efficacy, she replied, "I can do everything! It's in my Self, my successes, my environment, within me" (Navan, 2009, p. 67).

The young women demonstrated efficacy in a variety of ways—intellectually, emotionally, and behaviorally. Intellectually, all the girls were in accelerated learning environments, taking challenging advanced courses, in which they set high academic goals for themselves. Emotionally, they believed in themselves and demonstrated that they were capable of coping with difficulties and learning from them. Behaviorally, they showed that they could act in ways that reflected their authentic Self in different environments.

In my struggle to go back to school for an advanced degree in late life and in an area of study completely new to me, I approached a nearly complete loss of efficacy. Memorizing new material took much more effort that it did even as recently as when I studied for my doctorate in my late forties and early fifties. Learning and applying observational and therapeutic skills often was easy since I was able to call on familiar frameworks from my life as an educator. At other times, learning and using what seemed to be stiff and unnatural protocols felt awkward and was almost painful. Perhaps most significant was the diminishing energy I felt. I wondered where I would find the physical resources to complete hours and hours of a statistics assignment with a computer program that baffled me, or to study for a social psychology exam that my fellow graduate students, who were able to function on much fewer hours of sleep than I required, were able to accomplish much more quickly.

When health problems slowed me down, I asked myself frequently why would I, with a decent retirement and at a time in my life when I could take it easy, put myself through such stress and misery? Then I would remind myself that I had set a goal and who I am as an individual is someone who works to accomplish her goals. Additionally, I realize that were it not for several people, I would never have re-discovered my sense of efficacy. First, I have a spouse who continued to support my efforts and knew when to push a little to help me get back on track. Second, some of my professors, especially my thesis director, went way beyond what was required of them in assisting me in my learning. Finally, the other, younger graduate students were kind, open, welcoming, and encouraged my efforts.

Self-efficacy and the Aging Process

How is my story like the aging process for gifted elders? As we age, our bodies and our minds often diverge. Our minds continue to search for new learning and want to continue our creative productivity. Heilbrun (1997) describes life as we age as a time that opens for us, leaving us at liberty and eager to engage our creative spirit. At the same time our health and our physical capabilities may often curtail or limit those efforts. It is so sad for me when

I visit some of "my ladies" in residential care facilities whose minds are still quite active, yet they are limited by the confines of a sparsely furnished room and a dayroom that offers no intellectual stimulation.

> *It is only past the meridian of fifty that one can believe that the universal sentence of death applies to oneself.*
>
> (May Sarton, in Heilbrun, 1997, p, 75)

As mentioned previously, depression is common in aging individuals with cognitive impairment, illness, or disability. All three conditions are prevalent among the aging. Self-efficacy can be a robust mediating factor for a population at risk of developing mental health difficulties (e.g., depression, anxiety). A study of 160 aging individuals found that those with stronger self-efficacy in terms of their ability to control their environment demonstrated better mental health (Singh, Shukla, Singh, 2010). Other research indicated a positive association of memory self-efficacy with everyday memory performance among older males. In addition, the higher the self-efficacy score, the lower the anxiety (McDougall & Kang, 2008). Another study found that volunteering increased self-efficacy and decreased depression (Helmes & Govindan, 2007).

These studies confirmed self-efficacy is an important factor in healthy aging.

Given these findings, it was uplifting to read of self-efficacy beliefs in the narratives of the elders in my own research. In reflecting on her elderhood beyond 75 and into her nineties, Alicia wrote, "I intend to still be creating, writing, and interacting with a variety of individuals in an effort to continue learning and staying vital, while supporting others to do the same." Kate had completed an information technology degree course at age 55. She shared, "I guess my perspective toward myself has changed in that I am more confident in myself and in my gut feelings about things."

Amelia, at 59, is poised for efficacious aging as she revealed high self-efficacy merging into strong self-agency. In fact, she paraphrased the construct of self-agency when she wrote that she feels she recently gained confidence in her understanding that life is not something that happens *to* the individual. Rather, she expressed that she can control and choose the change or ignore what life may present to her.

Efficacious Aging

For readers who regularly interact with gifted elders, what supports could be offered to help them to continue to feel efficacious in a world where their dwindling capabilities and loss of personal freedom are ever present? We return to the concepts of intellectual, emotional, and behavioral efficacy.

Intellectually

When visiting gifted elders, family and friends can engage them in conversation that allows them to call on their strengths. If the elder was a nurse, ask him or her about some of the most enjoyable or intriguing cases. If you know music lovers, bring in recordings of favorite composers and ask them to teach you about the piece. Intellectually stimulating conversation, books, and other resources, and giving them the opportunity to share their knowledge will reinforce efficacy.

Remember that a central characteristic of giftedness is the rage to learn everything about a subject of interest. Family and others can tap into expressed interests by bringing and sharing new learning materials in the form of books, periodicals, tablet computers that allow access to course materials, and even experts who might be willing to visit gifted elders. Currently, I am in the process of developing a gifted elders speakers series in our community in which seniors and other experts in diverse fields will present talks on subjects of interest (e.g., foreign affairs, history, the arts).

Emotionally

One of the residents I visit regularly is confined to a wheelchair. Other than some memory difficulty, my friend is alert and conversational. She is a very gracious person and always a pleasure to visit. Her room is a refuge in an otherwise depressing residential care facility. During our visits I ask her to share her emotional strengths with me, thus reinforcing her emotional efficacy. If there is something that is bothering her during a visit, we talk about how she has coped with similar difficulties in the past. Her memories spark a problem-solving process, reminding her of coping strategies she can apply to the present.

Our wise elders are also excellent sources of support and advice. Bringing our concerns to them gives them the opportunity to share their wisdom and coping skills with us. Our inviting them to share their knowledge and expertise reinforces their own sense of feeling valued. In these instances, it is important to be authentic and carry through with their suggestions to the degree that it is practical. We should also be mindful of sharing difficulties in such a way that we do not cause them extra stress or anxiety.

Behaviorally

It is important to encourage our gifted elders to sustain their physical strength and mobility. If they are capable, walking through the halls of the residence, going out to a porch or garden, are ways to encourage activity. Often visitors are the only ones who suggest these activities and by doing so, they are reminded that they are capable and perhaps they will initiate the activities on their own or with others. Some readers will be able to share their physical conditioning skills with elders. Offering yoga, stretching, strength and resistance training, or meditation to the extent that our loved ones can participate are excellent pursuits.

Our life journeys are filled with experiences of efficacy, lost and regained. Assisting our gifted elders in regaining a sense of efficacy will increase their quality of life significantly. Additionally, in sharing our time and skills with elders, we model ways in which others and other generations can provide loving, supportive interaction when appropriate.

Part Two:
Aspirations

Chapter Six

Bucket Lists and Goal Setting: A New Perspective

The woods are lovely, dark and deep. But I have promises to keep, and miles to go before I sleep.

~Robert Frost

Among my preferred thought-talk show hosts are National Public Radio's Terry Gross and Diane Rehm. The interviews and conversations with authors, actors, musicians, political leaders, and others always hold my interest and leave me feeling that I have engaged in a worthwhile listening activity. A few years ago, hearing that Ms. Rehm was retiring left me feeling a bit sad and surprised. I wonder if others among the 2.4 million listeners that tuned into her show each week felt likewise.

In truth, I had no idea that Ms. Rehm has reached the age of seventy-nine. Yes, her voice sounded older, but I always thought that was due to spasmodic voice dysphonia disorder, which she suffered with for years. Otherwise, she was alert, vibrant, and by no means showing any signs of cognitive aging.

When I heard Steve Inskeep on *Morning Edition* speak with Diane Rehm about retirement, what caught my ear was her continuing zest for life and list of future projects. She shared that she planned to work through the upcoming 2016 presidential campaign, and that after retiring from her show, she would advocate for a cure for Alzheimer's and Parkinson's, create a series of podcasts, and more. "Voila!" I told my inner self, "A gifted elder's bucket list!"

A Qualitative Difference

The concept of bucket lists is not a new phenomenon—the To Do list of tasks one wants to accomplish before one passes has been popularized in films, blogs, and other media. For some, popular wishes include activities such as visiting the Acropolis, skydiving, or kayaking down the Amazon. While these and similar wishes are understandable, it is my belief that gifted elders have lists that, even though they may include some of the same activities, are qualitatively different.

Age-wise, I share the same decade as Diane Rehm, although unlike her I have not yet reached the cusp of eighty years. My life has been full as well as fulfilling. During my eight decades, I have known the love of a good man, shared the joys of raising children, held our grandchild in my arms, written, enjoyed three (yes three!) rewarding professions, delighted in traveling, and lived in three different countries and many different states. Yet, I still have a bucket list and it continues to grow. And I suspect that the experience of many gifted elders is the same.

What does a gifted elder's bucket list look like? At the top of the list of our gifted elders is the desire to continue to learn, experience, and grow spiritually. For example, Kate wants to see more of the world and to develop her musical side. Lana's bucket list includes learning a second language, authoring a book, and more travel. Other elders echo similar desires.

The qualitative difference with the bucket lists of gifted elders is rooted in several traits of gifted individuals. A primary characteristic of the gifted is the construct of asynchrony. Essentially, the term indicates that many gifted individuals do not develop in a stair-step fashion as described by common stage theories (e.g., Piaget, Erikson), where one stage naturally follows the other. Rather, in the gifted, we often see leaps of cognitive growth in one or more area of learning that are not accompanied by the same surge of social or emotional development. In a young gifted child, we might observe a seven-year-old who thinks on the level of a fourteen-year-old but has emotional meltdowns similar to the frustration tantrums of a three-year-old. Or we may observe emotional empathy and understanding beyond a child's years.

In terms of late adulthood, Erik Erikson's stage theory of development describes how individuals progress psychosocially from the stage of generativity, in which our creative productivity is at its zenith (usually during the years 40 to 65), to integrity, where we review our lives and see ourselves as accomplished and prepare ourselves for our final years (65 and beyond) (Erickson, 1994). In gifted elders, however, because of their asynchrony and coupled with the intellectual imperative of giftedness, the aging gifted may experience a mix of these stages beginning even earlier and continuing throughout the lifespan. We should not be surprised then, when our aging parents or friends demonstrate strong generativity as they continue to pursue or begin new projects of intellectual and creative interest late in life.

It has been my pleasure for during the past 50 years to work with gifted individuals. Early on, I realized that gifted behavior consists of the blending of three constructs, strong intellectual ability, goal-directed task commitment, and the need for creative productivity. These behaviors will persist in our gifted elders and we must continue to nurture and to celebrate them.

Goal Setting

In my early seventies I expressed the desire to walk El Camino de Santiago, the Way of St. James, in Spain in my seventy-fifth year. That is a fairly lofty goal for that age. Yet others in their eighth and ninth decades have done the nearly five-hundred-mile trek. However, I am sure that they were in much better health and physical condition than I was. I did not meet that goal due to health difficulties. However, the process of re-evaluating and revising the goal is in progress.

Goal setting differs from bucket lists. A bucket list is more like a wish list in that we express a desire to one day experience something (e.g. travel, activity). Bucket lists usually involve no specific plans until it becomes a goal. The example above—walking the Camino de Santiago—was a bucket list item for many years until I transformed it into a goal. A goal is an item that we can break down and organize as a list of steps to be accomplished toward the completion of the overall objective.

Goal Setting for Gifted Elders

In my view retirement can be a precarious time for seniors. Many look forward to the years following a life of work as a time that they will be able to do "all those things I never had time to do before." Yet, the same individuals may look back after 10 or 15 years of retirement and realize that yes, perhaps they spent a bit more time with family and maybe they traveled a little. Nevertheless, the plans they made upon retirement remain unaccomplished and they find they cannot account for how they spent the time.

Other retirees begin an entirely new venture in their senior years. They may choose as I did, to return to school and retool themselves for a new type of work. Or, they may begin a business, develop their artistic talents, or pursue any number of new activities fulltime. Aging in the post-retirement years is a regenerative time for many gifted elders.

What is the difference between the two groups? I am sure there are many variables that play into the life course of each individual and which affect one's productivity. Changes in the family structure, financial consequences, health difficulties, and other unexpected events can bring one to reassess and rearrange priorities. Nonetheless, it is my belief that, foremost among the differing factors in determining goal setting and goal accomplishment is self-regulation.

In *Nurturing the Gifted Female* (Navan, 2009), I wrote of the need for gifted females to develop self-regulation—the ability to set goals, to understand how one learns and accomplishes tasks, to organize oneself in such a way to complete those tasks successfully, and the capacity to judge when one is successful in reaching goals. Self-regulation is also an important construct in the lives of gifted elders. Some important self-regulation skills include organizing tasks, managing time conscientiously, efficiently planning and revising work as needed, and reflecting on and improving needed skills.

The most important behavior for self-regulated individuals is, in my opinion, effective goal setting. There are three facets to meaningful goal setting—planning long-term, short-term, and proximal goals. For the young females in my research, long-term goals might represent those accomplishments that one wanted to achieve in, for example, a year, two years, or 50 years in the future. Because of age and time concerns, this process looks quite different in elderhood. In my own case, even five-, 10-, or 15-year goals are quite tentative. For all of us, our time on the planet is finite and for some of us, the finiteness of time is inescapably clear. So, how do we go about goal setting as a part of the aging process?

A Goal is a Journey, and Nothing Else

Goal setting is especially important for those who find themselves transitioning from a busy professional life to the more relaxed agenda that retirement might offer. It is also vital that individuals continue to set and pursue goals throughout the aging process. I offer a process of backward planning as a method for gifted elders to set and accomplish goals.

A few weeks ago, I spent an afternoon thinking about goals and what amount of time might remain for me to achieve them. Knowing that during the past year or two many good friends and colleagues passed on, it is a sobering reflective experience to realize that one might pass at any time. At most, I have a couple of decades remaining in my life. Thus, I tried to picture what I would like to be doing 20 years from now. The activities that came to mind were simple and fitting with what my age will be at that time (my nineties). I want to find myself at leisure to read, walk, and write poetry.

My 15-year goals were similar—spending time with my spouse, reading, walking, and writing. As the years from the present into the future diminished, I added other activities. For example, within five to 10 years, I plan to have published three additional books and walked a good portion of the Camino. During the current year, my professional goals are for this book to be published, to renew my psychological associate license, and to start my next book. These are my long-term goals.

The next step in goal setting and planning is to look at each long-term goal and break it down into short-term goals. For example, knowing my current fitness and health, it would not be reasonable for me to try to walk the entire Camino in my eighties. In addition to distance, there are mountainous parts that could not be achieved. I must consider the maximum distance that can be completed in the time that I can allot. A bit of research will show me what part of the Camino suits my needs. Next, what season will be best for walking in that region? I find it important to assign a deadline by which I will have completed studying each topic of research. A vital part of goal setting is considering deadlines as sacred.

Now that I have my long-term and short-term goals set, the next part of the process is taking each short-term goal and enumerating the action items or tasks necessary to complete the goal. These are the proximal (next step) goals or tasks. Continuing with my example of the Camino, I list necessary tasks to completion, such as a progression of fitness training, travel arrangements, clothing and other gear. I then note on my calendar the completion date for each task.

With a backward planning process, one can develop each of the long-term goals and integrate the tasks for accomplishing them into day-by-day planning, gratifying the gifted individual's need for achievement and self-actualization. Gifted elders who have not made concrete plans prior to retirement, who are in residential facilities, who are in early stages of dementia, or face other challenges, may need assistance in identifying and ordering their goals, organizing themselves to meet their goals, and acquiring adequate materials to achieve their goals. Caregivers, family, and friends can all be of assistance in helping them to set and accomplish goals. If you have a gifted elder friend in similar circumstances, spending time talking with her about her dreams for the time remaining is the first step. Afterward, follow a goal setting and planning process. You can be valuable in supporting your friend in planning and living joyfully over the years.

Chapter Seven

The BE-attitudes of Gifted Elders

We have to make myths of our lives. It is the only way to live without despair.

(Sarton, 1996, p. 151)

Goal setting, as explored in the previous chapter, presents a method for gifted elders to plan their remaining years in such a way that they feel a sense of satisfaction and accomplishment. The *BE-attitudes* offered in this chapter, much like the biblical Beatitudes, move us from goals to dispositions. The term disposition connotes a temperament, a stance, and an internal impetus to action that reflect the character and values of an individual. I choose to think of dispositions as BE-attitudes because they are perspectives that convey a sense of commitment to a way of being consistent and integral to who the individual is and how the individual chooses to be.

> *Some of it's magic, some of it's tragic*
> *But I had a good life all of the way.*
>
> from *He Went to Paris*, by Jimmy Buffett

Be Present to Gratitude

The first BE-attitude disposition is being present to gratitude. During these elder years, my spouse and I remark often on how fortunate our lives have been. We have a marriage that has endured for over 45 years despite many health and other difficulties, we have two wonderful sons and their families, and we had the opportunity to develop fulfilling careers. Yes, we are grateful. However, do we cultivate the disposition of being truly present to gratitude? And what is gratitude and what does it mean to be present?

Gratitude is defined as a feeling of thankfulness. Mere thankfulness does not explain the depths of feeling many gifted individuals can experience. For myself, gratitude is the feeling that overwhelms me when I behold the awesome grandeur of Nature, my spouse, my grandchild, or any number of moments in my day when the beauty of my existence washes over me in continuous, unrelenting waves.

What does it mean to be present? It is to be here, now. Currently, younger generations enter elderhood indoctrinated by a culture of busyness and multitasking. However, the reality is that our brain is not wired to multitask. Rather, we are wired to attend to one stimulus at a time. Thus, being present to gratitude is attending, and attending, and attending, in a succession of moments. Michael Formica (2011) suggested a number of steps that assist us in being present, thus allowing us to cultivate the BE-attitude of being present to gratitude. To paraphrase him, they are:

- Breathing at a slow and deliberate pace, focusing on the outbreath.
- Practicing awareness of the present moment: where you are, what your thoughts are, what you are feeling.
- Being a witness to yourself and what you are doing in the present moment.
- Letting go of whatever is not in the present moment.
- Returning to the breath when something pulls you away from the present moment. Inhale slowly, breathe out, focus on the outbreath.

Elders who nurture gratitude in themselves experience numerous health benefits. Researchers note that in addition to improved psychological health, gratitude positively impacts physical health. In turn, sleep habits, self-esteem, and resilience—all problematic in elderhood—improve as well (Morin, 2014).

In my practice, I employ several strategies to assist my clients in developing and maintaining gratitude. A few of the strategies include:

- **Be open to the serendipitous.** Every day we are surrounded by surprises, gifts that we can notice or see in a new way if we are mindful of them. Scanning our environment may present a new blossom, a cloud formation, or the way the sun ripples through the trees and across the grass. Each phenomenon can bring us to an exclamation of gratitude if we open our minds to it.

In a similar vein, Grace, a member of our Council of Elders, wrote,

> *Sometimes I find myself "asleep at the wheel" of my life, going through the motions. But far more often I am awake to the discomfort and/or beauty of the present moment. By being awake, I can watch the emerging shoots that push through the soil from a house plant, and I can thank them for showing me the power and grace of life. I can hear the words of the young, gifted clients who see me as an ally who is in the NOW with them and not distracted by technology or my egoic mind. I can feel the hug of a grandchild who asks me if I knew she missed me while she was at pre-school.*

- **Keep a gratitude journal.** I encourage clients to use a gratitude journal to lift their mood. The smallest action or event can elicit our recording it. A statement like "Today I am grateful for" can precede a list of entries: a gentle rain, a visit from a friend, or other simple details of the day. Writing in the journal prior to bedtime may enhance sleep as well.

- **Focused breathing.** In therapy sessions I often spend time with clients, teaching them how to engage in focused breathing in which they become mindful of the air entering their nostrils, filling their lungs, and gently exiting as they breath out. Often, I combined their focused breathing with a habit I named Z-I-N breathing (Navan, 2009). Z-I-N is an acronym for "zero in now." As clients expel the first, deep breath, they relax their head and neck area. With the second breathing out, they relax head, neck, arms, and trunk. Finally, with the third exhalation, I direct them to relax "from the tip of the head to the tip of the toes."

  Z-I-N can be used at any time during the day and practiced without calling attention from others. I ask those clients I deem would benefit from practicing gratitude (and is there any of us who would not benefit?) to silently state to themselves something for which they are grateful as they release each breath.

Looking forward toward our 20 or 30 remaining years, the desire to experience gratitude with depth and palpability can only come from showing up and being present. In other words, rather than just "paying lip service" to gratitude, we can choose to live in such a way that exudes the gratefulness we feel for all of the gifts—of people, of nature, and of our own development—that we experienced throughout our lives.

If during our remaining 20 years we spend simply 15 minutes a day saying, "I am grateful," we have the potential to accumulate about three months of gratitude during those years. If we develop a habit of being continuously present to gratitude, we multiply that time exponentially.

As we age, countless negatives may confront us, such as impending death, diminished physical and mental health, limited financial resources, or loss of loved ones. It is no surprise then that so many elders are at risk of developing mood disorders. We learn from research that gratitude is one of the best defenses against mood disorders (e.g., depression, anxiety) and existential angst. Due to their heightened sensitivities, gifted elders have an increased likelihood of experiencing the extremes of sadness and of joy much more intensely.

It is my hope that all our elders have caring family and friends who help them to awaken the presence of gratitude. As Carla, a creative and highly gifted elder, wrote, "I am grateful for each day and wake with the wish of wanting to make the world a better place." In being present and practicing gratitude, it is my belief that gifted elders will find more contentment and pleasure in their lives. I am here. I am here now, and I am grateful.

Be Open to Finding Your Tribe

The second BE-attitude for gifted elders is to find your tribe. When I was a resource teacher for gifted students, I ensured that our students had the opportunity to be with like peers as much time during the school day as could be managed. Their intellectual and emotional well-being depended on their interactions with others who shared their abilities, their passion for learning, as well as their sensitivities and intensities. The placement of gifted students using the "sprinkle" method (placing one in one classroom and perhaps a couple in another) was tantamount to malpractice in my view. Besides not having academic needs met by teachers who could not or did not plan for the progress of the one or two gifted in the classroom, the social and emotional needs were almost certainly neglected as well.

Many of us have spent our childhood thinking that there was something wrong with us because we were so different from other children, not recognizing that it was our giftedness that made us feel so isolated.

When we did have the chance to congregate with others like ourselves, it was a joy to feel included. For many gifted individuals, that time does not occur until late high school, college, or beyond.

Where do you feel most included: at home, in church, with your community, with other gifted individuals, with multiage groups, in diverse settings? Adults have the freedom to choose our friendships and we tend to gravitate toward others who enjoy the same careers, hobbies, and other interests. Although difficult for many gifted adults, like peers are not impossible to find at work, in places of worship, or in our social activities.

What about our gifted elders? How do they find their tribe? I propose that, similar to younger technology-proficient counterparts, elders have the opportunity to consider their tribe as composed of between one and 7.7 billion individuals. They may prefer a community of one, a small group, large groups, or a global community.

Researchers inform us that in the gifted population introversion and extraversion are equally distributed (Cross, Cassady, & Miller, 2006). However, as intelligence increases, introversion increases also (Silverman, 1998). Thus, among gifted individuals with an IQ of 160, 75 percent are introverts. Consequently, we can surmise that many gifted elders may be content to be a tribe of one. They are gratified to pursue their interests and continued self-actualization without the need to socialize beyond a small group of family or friends. This is their privilege and a choice that needs to be honored and protected, especially in residential care facilities.

Too often I see introverts pressured to interact in settings that do not respond to who they are under the mandate of "socialization." We know that many early childhood educators oppose academic acceleration with the argument, which has been proven incorrect by research, that acceleration harms social development. In the same way, residential caregivers must understand that most gifted elders require quiet time alone and, unless they show clinical signs of depression or another difficulty, they deserve the choice to decline activities without sanctions or criticism.

My readers are probably asking why I would write that gifted elders may consider themselves members of a tribe of 7.7 billion, the current world population. Again, we to look to familiar characteristics of gifted children in order to understand the gifted elder. We know that most gifted children have a hunger to learn about their world, have a strong sense of justice, and are concerned about problems in the world. Those emotions do not disappear when childhood ends. My experience following the lives of the many gifted children whom I have taught and mentored demonstrates that when given the opportunity, gifted individuals possess a lifelong dedication to learning about their world and making it a more just, healthy, and peaceful globe.

Gifted elders have so much to share in this regard when given the chance to do so. As a dilletante in the arena of social media, I am impressed by the ease with which so many gifted elders (my social media tribe) know how to use the online environment to interact socially and in socially responsive ways. I belong to several groups of gifted adults. On one of the platforms, I belong to a forum created for each of us to share a triumph or a problem in confidence and receive appropriate responses and support. Some of us have shared our cancer journeys with other members and can attest to how their expressions of care fortified us and gave us a sense of peace in the midst of the turmoil. In the words of one participant, "Social media has been something of a godsend for this gifted introvert!"

Whether finding one's tribes means reaching out globally through technology to find like peers, or finding a small social group of intimate friends, or enjoying quiet, reflective time alone, the important aspect is that we as family, friends, and caregivers assist our elders in creating their special community.

Be Diligent in Cultivating a Spirit of Reverence

Several years ago, my husband and I took a nostalgic trip along Route 66 through the southwestern U.S.

While in the area, we took a side trip to Grand Canyon National Park, which I had visited in my late teens. At one point I miraculously found myself completely alone walking along the South Rim of the Canyon. I use the adverb "miraculously" because, unlike my visit more than 50 years before, one has a difficult time in this millennium finding a place of solitude on the South Rim. Yet for a few brief minutes I found that place. Walking along and pausing at the edge of the precipice, with no sound other than the ever-present wind sweeping along the canyon and the thunder in the distance, I was overcome with reverence. Reverence for the place—carved ribbons of varying shades of ochre, gray, and violet, with the scent of sage wafting on the breeze—and the ancients, whose spirits floated majestically and wisely in the air around me. It was an awe-filled moment.

Reverence is deep respect, approaching awe, a feeling or an expression of honor for someone or something. Along with other BE-attitudes of gifted elders like gratitude and finding your tribe, reverence requires bringing our gifted intensities to the moment and focusing our awareness on where we feel reverence. Below are a few of the phenomena in our lives which can spark feelings of reverence.

- **This day.** The older we are, the more we need to bring reverence to each day. Opening our eyes is a gift. Getting out of bed, beginning our day are all moments that we come to honor when we are more conscious that our days are numbered. When I bring my awareness to the first moments of the day, the words of one of my favorite poets come to mind.

> *i thank You God for most this amazing*
> *day: for the leaping greenly spirits of trees*
> *and a blue true dream of sky; and for*
> *everything*
> *which is natural which is infinite which is yes*
>
> (cummings, 1959, p. 114)

- **The natural world.** Each day that I am able, the first thing I do each morning is take a walk. Out the door and along our country road, I view the fields of soybeans that will soon make way for winter wheat, the line of trees with leaves changing to autumn colors, and the mackerel sky forecasting rain. The dew on the grass and the silence of the early morning air allow me to bring reverence to creation.
- **Emotions**. I am learning as a therapist that one of the first steps to healing is for my clients to realize that there are no bad emotions, there are just *emotions*. Thus, I must feel reverence for my anger as well as my joy, my fear of aging as well as my eagerness to see what happens next, my caution as I enter new paths as well as my trust that all will be well.

- **Pain**. Our son tells us of a drill sergeant he knew whose favorite expression was "Pain is weakness leaving the body." I believe that pain is a natural part of aging—at least for me it is. Thus, I can fight the pain of aging that I feel, or I can recognize it, honor it, let it go, and move on.
- **Solitude.** Most of my life I have been surrounded by people, both at home and in my work life. Now more often, my days are filled with solitude and recollection. Notice that I say solitude and not loneliness. Solitude is an interlude that can be revered. It is a time to do the mental work, the life review, that gives meaning to what came before and what is to come. It is a time to honor this day, our emotions, the natural world, and pain. It is blessed time.

There are many other reasons in our lives to feel reverence. This just skims the surface. Consider in what ways you express reverence in your life?

Be Persistent in Nurturing Your Poetic Soul

The past summer and early fall were a grace-filled time for me. Not only was I gifted with several weeks to spend with our treasured grandson, but I had the chance to re-connect with some very dear friends from years ago. The lives of the six members of their family life are interwoven with mine into cherished memories—as students, as friends, as participants in our wedding. Sheila, the eldest daughter, and I shared a lovely fall lunch in the beautiful Finger Lakes Region, after which she shared a poem with me, "Mindful" by Mary Oliver (2005, p. 58). The first few stanzas are below.

> *Every day*
> *I see or hear*
> *something*
> *that more or less*
>
> *kills me*
> *with delight,*
> *that leaves me*
> *like a needle*
>
> *in the haystack*
> *of light.*
> *It was what I was born for—*
> *to look, to listen*

The lines resonate with me because they leave me tingling with the beauty and grace of poetry as well as the joyful spirit with which each day should be lived. Sheila, one of our Council of Elders, personifies for me the gracious elder who lives each day in gleeful light.

In Chapter Two, we noted that gifted individuals may demonstrate one or more of several intensities which result in heightened awareness and experiences (Dabrowski, 2016). The intensities are intellectual, emotional, imaginational, psychomotor, and sensual. We see intellectual intensity in the child who buries himself in a subject in order to learn all he possibly can about it. Emotional intensity is apparent in the sensitivity and strong empathy we see in some gifted people. A child with psychomotor intensity is highly active and energetic. Children with this intensity are often at risk of being misdiagnosed with ADHD.

Individuals with imaginational and sensual intensities may feel the need to nurture their poetic souls on a regular basis. Imaginational intensity often is observed in those who have a rich inner life nourished by images and stories. Some choose to express their imagination through the arts. Others who experience sensual intensities may need to connect with Nature to feed their poetic soul.

One of our elders, Hannah, recounted that she took up piano at 40, belly dancing at 50, and beekeeping at 57. After 30 years in the city where she worked in a highly prestigious position, she moved to a house on the lake where she expects "more peace." Leigh, another elder, began writing poetry in her middle years after years of immersion in technology.

Other paths to nourishing our poetic souls are in music, art, or any of the creative worlds, whether natural or crafted by humans. I confess that I have not been nurturing my poetic soul much lately. I have not spent the time lost in words, or nature, or images. It takes the jarring of lines such as those above to bring me back to the hunger for literature that needs to be satisfied in order to restore my balance. In gratitude for the student who awakened it, I offer this as the fourth BE-attitude of gifted elders: nurture your poetic soul.

What about you? Do you feel as I do? How many times do we stop in the middle of a crowd and perceive the light resting softly on a branch, a blossom, or a sculpture? How often do we listen to the feelings forming words inside us that create the images and metaphors that describe the awe that we feel as a result of what we observe? When do we take the time to sit in the warmth of the waning autumn sun with the lines of our favorite poet before us? If you are held in the grasp of the present business of our lives, as am I, probably not often enough.

In my experience, poetry is a direct conduit to the depths of emotions, psychosocial development, and intellectual growth. This may not be true for all, since individuals have different strengths and intensities. Therefore, our gifted elders deserve the opportunity to access their emotions in different ways—through their hands, ears, or other senses, and through nature and the arts.

Be Resilient

I was privileged to work with Dr. Janice Leroux and assist her in the study of eminent Canadian women. Arising from interviews of 27 women who achieved excellence in the arts, social and physical sciences, engineering, and business, Leroux identified several psychological constructs (e.g., self-efficacy, self-agency) that contributed to the successful development and achievement of her participants (Leroux, 1994). Interestingly, in my study of gifted young females, I found many of the same constructs present at an earlier stage (Navan, 2009). Among the constructs of both studies was one that is crucial for successful aging in the gifted adult—resilience.

Resilience is the ability to bounce back in the face of difficulties. Picture a rubber band in its resting state as a metaphor for the gifted elder as she addresses everyday needs, engaging in problem-solving and future planning. Now imagine the rubber band being stretched to the point of breaking, equivalent to a gifted elder being stretched to her limit by the phenomena that accompany aging, such as sleep difficulties, or the aches and pains of aging muscles and joints, perhaps financial concerns, the loss of friends and loved ones, or even terminal disease.

At this point in our example, if one end of the rubber band is released, it snaps back into its original state. However, in the face of stress this snapping back in our gifted elders may not result to a return to the norm. Stress or trauma followed by a rapid return to status quo without processing the depth of the cognitive disruption may create conditions for acute or long-term stress. Thus, contrary to a rapid release of difficulty, resilience as it pertains to health is more a matter of using one's coping strengths to facilitate a softer easing of stress, creative problem-solving, and the recovery of a perspective of inner strength.

In their investigation "In resilience thinking, failure leads to growth," Edwards, Hall, and Zautra (2015) addressed resilience thinking in older adults, suggesting that appropriate coping and mind set skills can facilitate healthy acceptance of the declines of aging and the use of psychological strength necessary to move through losses and crises (Edwards et. al, 2015, p. 1). Such growth is a healthy outcome of resilience in individuals at all ages, but more so in the elderly, where crises and losses are often more frequent and numerous.

What does resilience look like in the gifted elder? Resilience is my brilliant ninety-year-old friend who, despite loss, frailty and pain, continues to review his important body of work, making sure that colleagues have the needed notes and analyses in their hands. Resilience is my friend, a university student in her sixties, reeling from a life of coping with trauma, who plans an affordable and sustainable residential living community for creative elders. Resilience is the health provider who, while healing from traumatic illness and surgery, spends hours "off the clock" supporting and allaying the fears of patients.

What are ways to foster resilience? Edwards and colleagues (2015) suggested that several characteristics and behaviors which foster resilience in elders include optimism, effective coping, personal connections, a sense of purpose, and self-efficacy. In addition, other aspects I have observed include gratitude, mindfulness, the opportunity to continue creative productivity, as well as a sense of wonder and appreciation for nature.

In my research and through my experience I found that self-awareness and understanding of emotions are two primary coping skills. Mindfulness is a practice which is hypothesized to promote self-awareness in the individual. For gifted elders, especially those experiencing early dementia, trained family and health workers can assist elders in the appropriate use of mindfulness. Early results of studies using mindfulness training with individuals with mild cognitive impairment or early dementia demonstrate improved cognition and reduction in memory loss (Berk, Warmenhoven, van Os, & van Boxtel, 2018).

The resilient gifted elder is one who stretches herself in response to stressful life events, always having within her the resources to gently relax, return to center, and regain a sense of awe and peace.

Be Mindful of Sanctuary

I am sitting beside a pool at a southern resort. Surrounding me are the sounds of children's voices, country music, quiet ripples, and the more insistent splashing of water. Yet the children's voices, country music, and splashing water do not distract, and the ripples serve as a soft accompaniment to my meditation. I am in sanctuary, a place I seek more often as I age. Sanctuary is a space that is a right of all gifted elders.

> *Aging, particularly in the last decades,*
> *is drawing in.*
>
> (Heilbrun, 1997, p. 57)

The word "sanctuary" connotes a sheltered, protected place. Not necessarily a physical place, it can be the placid inner space in which we rearrange the furniture of our mind to create harmony and quietude. Terry Hershey (2015), wrote in his book *Sanctuary: Creating a Space for Grace in Your Life* that finding sanctuary is intentional. It is a time when we search for the sacred in the ordinary, a time to refill our being with the essence of our spirit.

The lives of gifted elders are often filled with the directives of others, telling us to eat well, take it easy, not worry. As some gifted elders age, cognitive changes may cause them anxiety as they struggle to maintain an optimum level of functioning. Constant noise in the residential care environment contributes to difficulty in finding one's healing balance. These factors along with others highlight the need for gifted elders to find the restorative benefits that sanctuary offers.

Where can gifted elders find sanctuary? First and foremost, serene, natural settings can promote quieting of the mind, gathering of thoughts, and engaging in soul care. Gifted elders mention choice spots for reverie, such as a front porch or a deck, beside a river or lake, a bench in a clearing of a local park or arboretum, or while walking along a beach. Where do you find sanctuary?

Even without access to the natural world, sanctuary is an intentional choice that we make, even more so as we age. There, we can sort out the realities of aging and process the losses of friends and family. We can come to accept the physical and mental losses that aging brings. In sanctuary elders can learn to acknowledge the *never-agains* along with the gifts of elderhood, making peace with Self and the world.

Be Conscious of Leaving a Social Legacy

In Chapter Seven, we established that many aging gifted share the trait of introversion. In terms of an active social life, often the gifted elder spent a good part of adult life as a member of the smallest of social groups, the family. Socializing entailed the minimum of what was needed to satisfy the needs of the family unit. Other gifted individuals may have a small social group, preferring solitary pursuits over socializing.

Turning the subject over in my mind, I shifted the lens to observe other social actions of gifted elders. The change in perspective enabled me to understand their social impact. I came to perceive with more clarity the rich social gifts of gifted elders.

Among the dispositions—the BE-attitudes that enhance the lives of gifted elders—we observe the rich social legacy that many elders choose to leave as a result of their work for the common good in society. Despite their introversion and minimal socializing, we find gifted elders to be quite active in society. No, they are not your typical social butterfly, nor are they intent on adding friends and "likes" on social media. Rather, they are the quiet presence where tasks considered for the public good are accomplished.

Whenever I visit nursing homes, I see talented elders providing music, spiritual enrichment, playing games with residents, and involved in other activities.

Our team that prepares and serves food to the hungry at the local soup kitchen every month or two consists entirely of seniors, most of them gifted elders. I suspect that the makeup of most other teams is similar.

An acquaintance of mine and her spouse serve as surrogate grandparents for two children from an economically disadvantaged and dysfunctional family. They take the siblings to outings and for cultural enrichment each weekend, pay for a reading teacher to work with them in the summer, and otherwise provide needed support. I am sure they are just two of thousands of couples throughout the country who serve in this role.

A local group of quilters meets regularly to create beautiful quilts to present to newborns in the community. Local fish fry dinners, pancake breakfasts, spaghetti dinners, and other community events and fundraisers are staffed almost entirely by seniors. I have observed gifted elders working as volunteers at every blood donation event I have attended.

Our Council of Elders provides further examples of social legacy creation. Gifted advocacy ranks high among the group. In addition to their service in national and international gifted advocacy organizations, gifted elders mentor and coach gifted children, adolescents, and young adults. Others, such as David and Margaret, engage in environmental advocacy efforts. Several have recently become more politically engaged. Others are active in community service. In sum, our participants committed themselves to leaving a social legacy. In Sheila's words, "I would like to engage in activities through which I feel that I am true to my values and helping—in some small way—to make the world a better place, or at least life a little better for some people." Our gifted elders—when given the health, strength, and opportunity—continue to fulfill their blueprint, to evolve, and to contribute to the greater good.

PART THREE:
ADVOCACY

Chapter Eight

Creating Responsive and Differentiated Environments

I spend much time visiting elders in residential care facilities. The residents I visit represent a range of abilities and awareness. Nevertheless, as with all our elders, they all deserve the best care that we can provide for them according to their needs. Just as enlightened societies have come to realize that universal health care is a worthy goal to work toward, universal, quality eldercare is just as important a goal in such societies. Furthermore, just as gifted children deserve educational modifications that promote their optimal development, so also do *all* gifted elders, regardless of income, deserve caring, responsive settings that promote their continued well-being, enrichment, and optimal aging.

Four Elements of Differentiation

Four crucial elements contribute to the continuing enrichment and development in the lives of our elders. None would be cost-prohibitive to implement in any elder's home or residential care environment. Each element allows for a range of abilities and sensitivities, where individuals can pursue interests at their level of development, interest, and ability. The elements are integral to responsive and differentiated environments.

A Virtual Gifted Community

One of the curses of the elderly is loneliness, which manifests even more in our mobile, 21st century, where friends and family may live states, even countries, away from their elder's care facility. As more members of a technologically proficient generation age and enter residential care, these gifted elders will benefit from having access to technology, which will enrich their lives in numerous ways.

For example, video communication would allow gifted elders to interact regularly with family and others. Newer, more intuitive tablets would be relatively simple for most current seniors to master, even those with no technical background. Imagine what pleasure it would bring our older family members and friends to experience the regular video conferencing time that many of us as parents and grandparents appreciate. One friend's family lives in South America. They connect via Skype, and then leave the camera on while the children are playing, giving the grandparents and other relatives the chance to delight in their antics. I would have loved to have had the same opportunity when my children were growing up in the 1980s, 3,000 miles away from their grandparents. Video conference applications are becoming more user friendly, making connecting with loved ones via video as easy as answering a phone call.

A virtual gifted community would also allow gifted elders to continue connecting and collaborating with friends and colleagues through email and document sharing. Furthermore, with access to computers, elders can pursue diverse interests, study new subjects with MOOCs (massive online open courses), learn a new language, along with countless other enrichment activities. In short, providing a few computers in the day room of a facility or having touch sensitive tablets available to check out will provide elders with connection, communication, and continued cognitive growth—all benefits of a virtual community.

Literacy Rich Environment

I had the privilege of visiting Mary prior to her passing. She was introverted, seldom left her room, and always had a book in front of her. A member of her family arranged for her to receive boxes of books periodically on loan from the public library. If she finished a box before another replaced it, she would read some of the books again until a new box arrived. Mary would always brighten when I asked her about her reading, and she shared that she was hyperlexic and learned to read on her own as a preschooler, an early trait of giftedness.

Unfortunately, other than in Mary's room, I observed few books in that facility or in the other eldercare residences that I visit. Print material is limited to a few newspapers and trade magazines. However, there were other residents who asked me to bring newspapers or other media.

Effective educators acknowledge the importance of literacy rich environments for young learners. Ready access to books and other print materials and accessible writing materials for composition give students a learning advantage. In fact, books in the home is a prime factor in students' later achievement. In the same way, our bright, gifted elders who have spent their lives with books need settings that include the elements of literacy.

What would eldercare facilities that are literacy rich environments look like? We need only look at what reading experts promote for early readers.

- They would have a library with a variety of genres of books available in standard print and large type, Braille, online, and audio-formats. These materials would stimulate conceptualization and creativity, along with providing for reading enjoyment.

- Print media would abound throughout. Additionally, writing centers with computers, paper, and adaptive writing utensils would be offered where elders can compose and, if they choose, display their work.
- Facilities would offer visits by local authors who would give book talks. Book groups where elders could read and discuss their reading together would be scheduled.
- Directors would provide quality creative materials (not just craft materials) across disciplines that promote continued creative productivity. Pastels, sculpting clay, musical staff, and drawing paper are some examples.

Our gifted elders need more than a day room with jigsaw puzzles and a television. They need the opportunity to continue to engage their minds in thoughtful activities that can only be accomplished in literacy rich environments.

Freedom to Self-Regulate

The third element in responsive and differentiated environments for gifted elders is the freedom to self-regulate to the greatest extent possible within the confines of institutionalized care. Acknowledging that there must be a certain clarity of protocol and scheduling that eldercare staff members must adhere to, I suggest that latitude be granted for our gifted elders to find their own rhythm within their new environments.

Once when visiting a friend in an assisted living/ eldercare home, one of the aides came to her suite while we were in the middle of a deep and meaningful conversation. "Wakey, wakey," the aide said, "time for a shower." Then, when my friend said she had a visitor and asked if she might be able to shower later, the aide began to make silly movements, acting out scrubbing under the arms and speaking to her as if she were an infant. Soon it was clear that we were not going to be able to continue our work until the aide completed her *duty*. I was saddened that my friend, one of the brightest people I know, was being treated in such a degrading fashion. Yet, similar behavior is not unusual at present, where our elders, far from being respected and revered, are often seen as objects to be washed, clothed, fed, and told to rest and not make a disturbance; and all on a strict schedule.

What might responsive environments that ensure elders the freedom to self-regulate look like? First, caring administrators and staff members will respect individual choices to the greatest extent possible. In other words, my friend whose social visit was rudely interrupted could have been asked, upon seeing that she had a visitor, when she would be available for the aide to return. Diet provides another opportunity for freedom to self-regulate. In some, but not many facilities, individuals may select menu items within the structure of a well-balance meal, providing them choice while meeting their nutritional needs.

Some of the residences I visit offer a *one-size-fits-all* activity schedule. A step toward allowing for self-regulation would be to offer choices of activities, rather than the same activity for all residents. While some might enjoy bingo, others might prefer word games or checkers or chess. In day rooms, in addition to jigsaw puzzles, having activities on hand that encourage intellectual and creative risk-taking, such as 3-D puzzles, problem-solving games, and crossword puzzles or anagrams, give high-functioning elders the opportunity to engage in more cognitively stimulating activities.

Elder gifted individuals are often introverts and need solitude, time for reading or individual creative work. As regulations allow and to the extent that it is healthy for them, they should have the option of choosing times when they will not be disturbed or forced to join group activities. Along that same line, as much flexibility as possible in scheduling will promote positive self-regulation as well. Being able to choose from two dining hour options, having the opportunity to be outside in the natural environment, negotiating times for showers and other hygiene with the staff, presenting themselves at the dispensary for medications without having their names called on a PA system—all of these are examples of how our cognitively aware elders, who may, due to health or financial circumstances, be confined to basic residential care, can continue to enjoy the dignity and respect they deserve.

A Space for Spiritual Enrichment

No matter what our beliefs, we all encounter what my friend and mentor, Annemarie Roeper, termed "the mystery." It might be the sense of wonder we felt as a child the first time we saw a star-filled summer night sky. For some perhaps, the birth of a child inspired it. For others, the overwhelming aesthetic wonders of a Mozart symphony, or a painting by Van Gogh or da Vinci may precipitate it. The encounter with *the mystery* also takes the form of spiritual enlightenment or connection, both while alone and with others.

The hunger for connection and enlightenment may be even more crucial for individuals as they age. As responsibilities for work, family, and other tasks drop away, elders find themselves entering a stage of life described by Erikson (1994) as that of *Integrity vs. Despair*. We contemplate the path of our lives thus far, hopefully gaining wisdom from our past endeavors, and begin to seek a sense of satisfaction and wholeness as we prepare for death without dread. To enrich and sustain contemplation, elders need settings that promote opportunities for spiritual reflection and growth.

> *The most beautiful thing we can experience is the mysterious. It is the source of all true art and science. He to whom the emotion is a stranger, who can no longer pause to wonder and stand wrapped in awe, is as good as dead—his eyes are closed.*
>
> ~Albert Einstein (1985)

How might eldercare facilities respond to the needs of elders for environments that allow for their spiritual reflection and growth? First, residential care settings should have quiet spaces both indoors and in natural settings. The spaces should be designed to facilitate meditation, prayer, or other spiritual exploration. Water features such as indoor or outdoor fountains, plants, and art or sculpture may offer inspiration or a meditative focus. Soft lighting, natural if possible, and subdued colors will encourage quiet, restful reflection. Shapes and textures should be soft also. In short, glaring, loud, or sharp features may disturb the sensitivities and intensities that many gifted elders experience. Some find the availability of soft, meditative music—with the option of controlling the volume or turning it off—supportive of spiritual enhancement.

Reflective spaces should respect all spiritual frameworks, religious or otherwise. Thus, I would suggest avoiding overt and aggressive use of religious symbols. Incense or other aromas could be available for those who desire them. Books and meditative literature might be available, yet discreet. There should be seating arrangements for individual and group reflection. Above all, these spaces should be as *non-clinical* and natural as possible. Materials for recording thoughts and insights, and for journaling as one conducts a life review would be helpful. I would suggest that a capable staff member or volunteer may also be available at set times to assist in the life review process.

Additional Elements for Healthy Aging

Sundowner's, or *sundowning,* is a syndrome which manifests itself in many individuals with Alzheimer's disease or other dementia-related diseases. Changes in light at the end of the day may produce behaviors such as agitation and restlessness, anxiety, fear, or anger. Similarly, adults, and specifically elder adults, may present with sleep difficulties. Research demonstrates that seven of 10 older adults have sleep disturbances or sleep disorders. Due to the intensities of giftedness, I believe that the statistic may be higher with gifted elders.

As with sundowning, light and how our brains process light is often connected to problems falling asleep or difficulty staying asleep. Receiving different types of light at different times during the day or evening can support or disrupt the circadian rhythms that control our sleep drive. Circadian rhythms are necessary for promoting healthy sleep-wake cycles. When the natural rhythms are upset, we have trouble initiating, maintaining, and waking from sleep.

Researchers at the Light and Health Center of Rensselaer Polytechnic Institute have developed a light table that emits bluish-white light (i.e., daytime type), and they investigated its use in residential care facilities for the elderly. Residents gathered around the light table at meals and were free to sit at the table anytime between 6 a.m. and 7 p.m. After use of the table over time, caregivers recorded a 10 percent increase in sleep efficiency, the ratio of time in bed to time sleeping, among residents who used it. The less time they took falling asleep and the more time they stayed asleep, the better their sleep efficiency.

In addition to sleep efficiency, elders who regularly used light tables displayed a substantial decrease in depressive symptoms and agitation. This reinforces the importance of our elders receiving as much natural daylight as possible during the day, especially in the winter months. In addition, we should begin to eliminate unhealthy sources of light for two or more hours before bedtime.

Fibromyalgia is one of several disorders marked by fatigue and sleep issues. As an individual who has learned to manage fibromyalgia over four decades,

I have developed sleep rituals to help alleviate the sleep problems that are inherent with the disorder. The following are some of the techniques and rituals that elders may find to be helpful for falling asleep and enhancing beneficial, sound sleep.

- Reduce screen time in front of television and electronics in the evenings for at least two hours before bedtime. These devices emit bluish-white light, which promote wakefulness rather than sleepiness.
- Dim the lights at night a few hours before turning in for the night. This produces a calm, soothing environment for the gifted elder.
- If the older adult needs some light when getting up during the night, use a soft night-light placed at a strategic spot to assist in navigating the dark. Some residential facilities now use softly lighted door frames, rather than bright hallway lights. Soft lights guide residents safely without encouraging wakefulness.
- Find an activity that helps the gifted elder wind down at the end of the day. It may be reading with a small reading light, sketching, knitting, doing a jigsaw or word puzzle that is not overly challenging, or listening to relaxing music. Any type of quiet activity that can be developed into a nighttime ritual will serve

as a trigger, telling one that it is time for the mind and body to prepare for sleep.

- Sounds from nature, ocean waves, rain, or ripples from a stream are relaxing and useful as sleep aids. One of the treasured gifts from a son who understands my sleep difficulties is a sleep sound machine that generates these and other natural sounds.
- Some find aromatherapy helpful. Lavender, chamomile, bergamot, and sandalwood are some scents that come to mind. A few drops of one of these essential oils on a cotton ball placed near one's pillow may be beneficial.
- Deep breathing, muscle relaxation, or guided imagery may be useful in falling asleep. I tap into scenarios of favorite places that I have visited—a restful beach, camping in the mountains, among others—and use them as guided imagery visualizations to relax and prepare me for sleep.
- Sleep experts tell us to try to go to sleep and to awaken at the same time every day. This sets up our natural circadian rhythm. Also, if a nap is needed during the day, limit it to a 15-minute or so power nap in the early afternoon.
- Exercise during the day is important. We need to exercise early enough during the day to

allow our bodies to cool down into a more sleep receptive state. For example, a good friend and colleague of mine is a runner. He found as he started to age that he had to switch the time of his afternoon runs to earlier in the day in order not to interfere with his sleep at night.

These are just a few of responsive elements that I offer for differentiating environments for our aging elders. I welcome your suggestions as well. Please post them on my site, www.ongiftedelders.com.

Chapter Nine
Looking Forward

> *The psyches and souls of women also have their own cycles and seasons of doing and solitude, running and staying, being involved and being removed, questing and resting, creating and incubating, being of the world and returning to the soul-place.*
>
> (Clarissa Pinkola Estes, 1996, p. 256-257)

A young client recently commented, "The schools won't change, so I guess I will have too." Thankfully I could assist him in developing the understanding that one does not have to "give up" giftedness, as if it were possible to do so. Rather, the student and I could work together with his parents to find resources and advocates within the system. If our search proved unsuccessful within that learning environment, we would find other ways or environments that supported his unique needs. What was important in our work together was for the gifted young person to come to understand and accept his exceptional abilities and his intensities. It is just as essential that gifted elders accept their exceptionalities and move forward.

Honor Self

We have seen in our participants that it was not until much later in life that many of them realized their giftedness and understood the sensitivity and intensity that the construct entails. They recalled the elementary, middle, and high school years during which they felt isolated and different much of the time. Not until their adult or elder years did they report feeling their authentic Self. For most of our Council of Elders, no one used the *G word* during their childhood. Understanding giftedness in their early years is something they wish they had understood back then.

When gifted elders recognize and appreciate the characteristics of giftedness (e.g., profound intellectual curiosity, emotional intensity, strong sense of justice), they learn to accept and honor Self. To honor Self involves accepting all facets of their being. Instead of regretting that we are "too much" in terms of feeling empathy so deeply that it is painful, we accept the pain, acknowledge it, and recognize it as a shining facet of our being, of who we are. Instead of feeling that we are "over the top" in our rage to know and understand our world, we appreciate our appetite for learning. Through gentleness and compassion, we honor these gifted aspects and others.

Solitude vs. Loneliness

Growing up as a shy, introverted reader and thinker in a family with three brothers, I spent much time alone, pursuing my own interests. I relished the time I had to read several books a week. A member of a free-range generation of children, I recall days when I would leave our house early morning and not return until evening, except for lunch. At times I joined my brothers or neighborhood children to play. However, often I would explore the woods and the creek behind our house, creating elaborate scenarios and stories with my imaginary friend, Beth.

Because of their introversion, many gifted adults preferred solitude as children. As they grew older, society's view impressed on them the expectation that they be more engaged in social activities. Perhaps they began to question their love of spending time alone. The message conveyed by teachers and other adults was that to be happy, one must have a bevy of friends with which to spend every waking moment.

It was not until young adulthood that I and some of our gifted elders realized the penchant for having just one or two close friends was perfectly acceptable. Furthermore, solitude was to be celebrated, especially since it allowed and fostered space for creative productivity. A vital task for gifted adults and elders is distinguishing solitude from loneliness.

Celebrate the Positives of Gifted Intensities

Growing up an empath who felt physical pain when others suffered, along with all of the intensities that mark many gifted individuals—sensual, imaginational, intellectual, emotional, and psychomotor—it was a mystery to me why I overreacted to stimuli when others did not. As with my preference for solitude, I interpreted my intensities as something wrong with me rather than something right.

Looking back on years of misinterpretation, had I known, I would have used the intensities to plow deeper into my quest for understanding of my world and others as well as my self-understanding. When we celebrate the intensities of gifted children rather than try to suppress them, we give them the freedom to feel deeply and to pursue their imaginational creativity. We affirm the intellectual imperative that drives their being and we do all we can to nurture it. Equally, we must recognize and celebrate the intensities of our gifted elders.

I Do What I Am

A quote attributed to Freud, "I do what I am," resonates strongly with my thinking. When I heard it, I thought, "Yes! That is my professional trajectory as well." In my thirties, when I began the journey of giftedness in education, I studied, wrote, and presented on best educational practices for gifted students. In my forties, I progressed into a doctoral program in educational psychology with a specialization in giftedness and my studies opened my mind to my own giftedness. Thus, my dissertation focused on gifted females. In my fifties and sixties, I was a college professor who wrote and taught about the psychology of the gifted. Now, in my seventies, I study and advocate for gifted elders. I do what I am.

What more does "I do what I am" require in order to live as a self-actualizing gifted elder? Essentially, I urge readers to continue to savor and to celebrate the astonishing miracle that is life, along with the exhilarating recognition that through life we are all connected to the ever-creative spirit of the universe. Some may choose to call that spirit Prime Mover or Creator God or one of a multitude of names. Regardless, we have been blessed with grace and gratitude for an intense awareness of our connection with creation. It is a connection that wraps us in love during some of the darkest moments and through the most painful days. Even when depressed, that connection remains if we just tap into it. As gifted elders it is our task to transform distress into an affirmation of life.

Furthermore, the Council of Elders personifies "I do what I am." They have renewed in me an understanding that we are tasked with helping others to experience joy as well. It can be as little as offering a smile, as Amelia shared. Hannah wrote about her gratefulness that she has "in fact changed a corner of the world." And Alicia expressed, "There's that whole changing the world thing." To leave our gifted contribution is to do what we are.

> *Our lives begin to end the day we become silent about things that matter.*
>
> ~Martin Luther King, Jr.

I grew up during a century when millions of men, women, and children were marginalized and murdered because of their ethnicity, religion, gender, sexual preference, or for any other reason that caused them to be deemed *dangerous* to malevolent and fascist leaders. Furthermore, during that time our own nation—the nation founded on the belief in the right of all (although, admittedly, for most of our history it has never been "all") to "life, liberty, and the pursuit of happiness"—established internment camps and isolated our own citizens because of their ancestry or ethnicity.

I am grateful for younger generations and for the gifted elders who taught them. They are more open to diversity. Learning from and celebrating the differences makes us stronger. Granted, there will always be malicious, radical elements. A task of "I do what I am" for gifted elders as keepers of the stories and memories is to continue to share the stories and memories of what humanity can be.

Appendix

Additional Resources

Books and Articles

Aron, E. N. (2020). *The highly sensitive person: How to thrive when the world overwhelms you.* Citadel.

Bateson, M. C. (2001). *Composing a life.* Grove Press.

Bateson, M. C. (2011). *Composing a further life: The age of active wisdom.* Vintage.

Bolen, J.S. (2014). *Goddesses in older women: Archetypes in women over fifty.* Harper.

Borysenko, J. (2009). *It's not the end of the world: Developing resilience in times of change.* Hay House.

Daniels, S. & Piechowski, M. M. (2009). *Living with intensity.* Great Potential Press.

Fiedler, E. D. (2015). *Bright adults: Uniqueness and belonging across the lifespan.* Great Potential Press.

Kerr, B. & McKay, R. (2014). *Smart girls in the 21st century: Understanding talented girls and women.* Great Potential Press.

Maisel, E. (2013). *Why smart people hurt: A guide for the bright, sensitive, and the creative.* Conari Press.

Mendaglio, S. (2008). *Dabrowski's theory of positive disintegration.* Great Potential Press.

Merrill, J. & Wilson, S. (Ed.). (2012). *If this is a gift can I send it back?: Surviving in the land of the gifted and twice exceptional.* GHF Press.

Neville, C. S., Piechowski, M. M., & Tolan, S. S. (Eds.), *Off the charts: Asynchrony and the gifted child.* Royal Fireworks Publishing.

Pinkola Estés, C. (1996). *Women who run with the wolves: Myths and stories of the wild women archetype.* Ballantine Books.

Prober, P. (2016). *Your rainforest mind: A guide to the well-being of gifted adults.* GHF Press.

Prober, P. (2019). *Journey into your rainforest mind: A field guide for gifted adults and teens, book lovers, overthinkers, geeks, sensitives, brainiacs, intuitives, procrastinators, and perfectionists.* Luminare Press.

Rinn, A. N. & Bishop, J., (2015). Gifted Adults: A systematic review and analysis of the literature. *Gifted Child Quarterly. 59*, 213-235.

Rivero, L. (2010). *A parent's guide to gifted teens: Living with intense and creative adolescents.* Great Potential Press.

Roeper, A. & A. Higgins (2007). *The "I" of the beholder: A guided journey to the essence of a child.* Great Potential Press.

Roeper, A. (2012). *Beyond old age: Essays on living and dying.* Azaela Art Press.

Silverman, L. K. (2013). *Giftedness 101.* Springer.

Tolan, S.S. (2016). *Out of sync: Essays on giftedness.* Royal Fireworks Press.

Webb, J. T. (2013). *Searching for meaning: Idealism, bright minds, disillusionment, and hope.* Great Potential Press.

Webb, J. T., Amend, E. R., Webb, N. E., Beljan, P., Webb, N. E., Kuzujanakis, M., Olenchak, F.R., Goerrs, J. (2016). *Misdiagnosis and dual diagnosis of gifted children and adults: ADHD, Bipolar, OCD, Asperger's, Depression, and other disorders.* Great Potential Press.

Journals and Newsletters

2e Twice Exceptional Newsletter. Articles regarding children and others who are gifted with learning disorders. May be of interest to adults and elders with similar development.

Advanced Development Journal. A journal devoted to adult giftedness.

Gifted and Talented International. Journal of the World Council for Gifted and Talented Children. Some articles on gifted adults.

Gifted Child Quarterly. Published by the National Association for Gifted Children (NAGC). Research and other articles about giftedness and talent development. Occasional articles on gifted adults.

Journal for the Education of the Gifted. Articles regarding gifted education and psychological needs of gifted individuals. Occasional articles on gifted adults.

Journals of Gerontology, Series B. Articles that address the biological and medical aspects of aging.

Roeper Review. Articles on giftedness with some on adult giftedness.

World Gifted. Newsletter of the World Council for Gifted and Talented Children (WCGTC).

Websites

2eresource.com. Resources for twice exceptional individuals.

Davidsongifted.org. The Davidson Institute was founded with the aim of nurturing and supporting the profoundly gifted. The database, davidsongifted.org/search-database, is a rich collection of articles and other resources for gifted individuals and professionals.

Facebook.com. Many groups for networking with other gifted adults and elders: Bright and Quirky, Dabrowski International, Embracing Intensity, Gifted Homeschoolers Forum Discussion Group, Gifted Unlimited, The Highly and Profoundly Gifted Group, This Chair Rocks, and more.

Giftedchallenges.blogspot.com. Psychologist Gail Post explores the social and emotional facets of giftedness.

Hoagiesgifted.org. The "all things gifted" page with resources for parents, professionals, and others.

Nagc.org. The website of the National Association for Gifted Children. Find how to connect to state organizations at http://www.nagc.org/information-publications/gifted-state.

Ongiftedelders.com. My blogspot, plus the home of Navan Consultation Services.

Rainforestmind.wordpress.com. The blogspot of gifted adult goddess, Paula Prober.

Sengifted.org. The home of the SENG organization, Supporting Emotional Needs of the Gifted.

Welcometothedeepend.com. For bright kids (and others) who S. Tolan describes as "too far from the norms to 'fit.'"

References

Andrus, M. (2016, January 11). Obituary for Lowell David Latto. *Murray Ledger & Times.*

Andrus, M. (2016, January 19). Obituary for Yancey Lee Watkins. *Murray Ledger & Times.*

Ban Breathnach, S. (1996). *The simple abundance journal of gratitude.* Warner Books.

Bandura, A. (1997). *Self-efficacy: The exercise of control.* W. H. Freeman and Company.

Berk, L., Warmenhoven, F., van Os, J., & van Boxtel, M. (2018). Mindfulness training for people with dementia and their caregivers: rationale, current research, and future directions. *Frontiers in Psychology, 9*, 982. https://doi.org/10.3389/fpsyg.2018.00982

Carter, J. (1998). *The virtues of aging*. Ballantine Publishing.

Clark, A.J. (2013). *Dawn of memories: The meaning of early recollections.* Rowman & Littlefield.

Cross, T.L., Cassady, J.C., & Miller, K.A. (2006). Suicide ideation and personality characteristics among gifted adolescents. *Gifted Child Quarterly, 50* (4), 295-306.

cummings, e.e. (1959). *100 selected poems*. Grove Press, 114.

Dabrowski, K. (1964, 2016). *Positive Disintegration*. Maurice Bassett.

Edwards, E.S., Hall, J., & Zautra, A. (2012, April). Resilience in aging. *Elder Care: A Resource for Interprofessional Providers.*

Einstein, A. (1985). *Living philosophies.* Creative Co.

Erikson, E.H. (1994). *Identity and the life cycle*. W.W. Norton and Company.

Fiedler, E.D. (2015). *Bright adults: Uniqueness and belonging across the lifespan*. Great Potential Press.

Formica, M.J. (2011, June 14). 5 steps for being present. *Psychology Today*. https://www.psychologytoday.com/us/blog/enlightened-living/201106/5-steps-being-present

Gilligan, C. (1982). *In a different voice: Psychological theory and women's development*. Harvard University Press.

Heilbrun, C.G. (1997). *The last gift of time: Life beyond sixty*. Ballantine Books.

Helmes. E. & Govindan, A. (2007). Differences between older adult volunteers and non-volunteers in depression and self-efficacy. *Australian Journal on Volunteering, 12* (2), 30-36.

Hershey, T. (2015). *Sanctuary: Creating a space for grace in your life.* Loyola Press.

Jackson, P.S. (2017). Gifted Adults, standing, like curious children, before the great mystery into which we were born...paraphrased from Einstein. *Daimon Institute.*

http://www.daimoninstitute.com/2017/02/04/gifted-adults-standing-like-curious-children-before-the-great-mystery-into-which-we-were-born-paraphrased-from-einstein/

Kaufman, S.B. (2018, November 7). Beautiful minds: What does it mean to be self-actualized in the 21st century? *Scientific American*. https://blogs.scientificamerican.com/beautiful-minds/what-does-it-mean-to-be-self-actualized-in-the-21st-century/

Kem, L. & Navan, J.L. (2006). Gifted students in college: Suggestions for advisors and faculty members. *NACADA Journal, 26* (2), 21-28. https://doi.org/10.12930/0271-9517-26.2.21

Lathem, E.C. (Ed.). (1969). Stopping by the woods on a snowy evening. *The Poetry of Robert Frost*. Henry Holt and Company, p. 224.

Leroux, J.A. (1994). A tapestry of values: Gifted women speak out. *Gifted Education International, 13*, 4-12.

Lovecky, D.V. (1986). Can you hear the flowers singing? Issues for gifted adults. *Journal of Counseling and Development, 64* (1986), 572-575.

Maslow, A. H. (1943). A theory of human motivation. *Psychological Review, 50*, 370–396.

Maslow, A.H. (1968). *Toward a psychology of being* (2nd edition). Van Nostrand Company.

McDougall, G.J. & Kang, J. (2008). Memory self-efficacy and memory performance in older males. *International Journal of Men's Health, 2* (2), 131-147.

Miller, J.B. (2012). *Toward a new psychology of women* (2nd edition). Beacon Press.

Morin, A. (2014, November 23). 7 Scientifically proven benefits of gratitude that will motivate you to give thanks year-round. *Forbes.* https://www.forbes.com/sites/amymorin/2014/11/23/7-scientifically-proven-benefits-of-gratitude-that-will-motivate-you-to-give-thanks-year-round/#144092d4183c

Morris, J. (2012, February 3). Obituary for William Franklin Wells. *Murray Ledger & Times.*

Nagaswami, V. (2016, October 10). All in the brain. *The Hindu.*

Navan, J. L. (2009). *Nurturing the gifted female: A guide for educators and parents.* Corwin Press.

Navan, J. L. (2013, January 23). 100 words of wisdom: Joy Navan. *SENG: Supporting Emotional Needs of the Gifted.* https://www.sengifted.org/post/100-words-of-wisdom-joy-navan

Obituary for Kenneth H. Theobald. (2016, October 9). *Burlington Free Press.*

O'Boyle, M.W. (2005). Some current findings on brain characteristics of the mathematically gifted adolescent. *International Education Journal 6* (2), 247-251.

O'Donohue. J. (1999). *Anam Cara.* Bantam Press.

Oliver, M. (2005). Mindful. *Why I wake early: New poems by Mary Oliver*. Beacon Press, 58.

Pinkola Estes, C. (1996). *Women who run with the wolves: Myths and stories of the wild woman archetype.* Ballantine Books.

Prober, P. (2016). *Your rainforest mind: A guide to the well-being of gifted adults and youth.* GHF Press.

Reynolds, C.F., Alexopoulos, G.S., Katz, I.R., & Lebowitz, B.D. (2001). Chronic depression in the elderly: Approaches for prevention. *Drugs and Aging, 18,* 507-514. https://doi.org/10.2165/00002512-200118070-00004

Roeper, A. (2007). *The "I" of the beholder: A guided journey to the essence of a child.* Great Potential Press.

Roeper, A. (2011). *Beyond old age: Essays on living and dying.* Azalea Art Press.

Sarton, M. (1996). *Plant dreaming deep: A journal.* W.W. Norton and Company.

Silverman, L.K. (Ed.). (1993). *Counseling the gifted and talented.* Love Publishing.

Silverman. L.K. (1998). Personality and learning styles of gifted children. In Van Tassel-Baska, J. (Ed.) *Excellence in Educating Gifted & Talented Learners* (3rd edition). Love Publishing Company.

Singh, A.P., Shukla, A., & Singh, P.A. (2010). Perceived self-efficacy and mental health among elderly. *Delhi Psychiatry Journal, 13,* 314-321.

Tolan, S. & Piecowski, M. (2013). Giftedness: Lessons from Leeuwenhock. In Neville, C.S., Piechowski, M.M., & Tolan, S.S. (Eds.). *Off the charts: Asynchrony and the gifted child.* Royal Fireworks Press.

Webb, J.T., Amend, E.R., Webb, N., Goerss, J., Beljan, P., & Olenchak, F.R. (2005). *Misdiagnosis and dual diagnoses of gifted children and adults.* Great Potential Press.

Acknowledgments

I wish to express my most sincere gratitude to the gifted elders whose voices gave life to this book. I will always be grateful for their willingness to share their Self and their stories in the hopes of helping other gifted elders as they experience aging. They are my heroes.

To the gifted elders who inspired my work I express my humble yet immense appreciation for their mentoring. Dr. Janice Leroux's work with eminent women inspired my own path to narrating the lives of gifted individuals. Her wise lessons continue to inspire my research and writing. Dr. Annemarie Roeper accepted me under her guidance and instruction despite her age and failing health. Her voice is forever in my ears gently encouraging and affirming my work. Evelyn Freeman Todd, my mother, was the first gifted woman in my life. She gave me the strength to explore new paths without regard to societal norms and expectations.

My editor, Sarah Wilson, has supported me through the journey of birthing this book and always expressed her belief in me. My voice is stronger thanks to her collaborative expertise. To my friend and publisher, Molly Issacs-McLeod, thank you for your care and tender guidance. Finally, to Lori Comallie-Caplan, who wrote the foreword to this book. You are a fiercely gifted warrior who will always inspire me.

About the Author

Joy L. Navan is a Licensed Psychological Associate and Educational Consultant at The Amend Group. As an LPA she provides assessment and therapy services for gifted children, adolescents, adults, and elders.

After almost three decades as a teacher of Spanish and a resource teacher for the gifted, Dr. Navan studied at the University of Ottawa and completed a Ph.D. with a specialization in giftedness. She began a second career as a professor of education. Upon retirement from Murray State University as professor emeritus, Dr. Navan was motivated to retrain as a psychological associate to meet the social, emotional, and educational needs of the gifted in the western region of Kentucky. With her advanced Spanish degree, Ms. Navan provides psychological services to the Spanish-speaking population as well.

Dr. Navan has extensive experience in facilitating acceleration of highly, exceptionally, and profoundly gifted students. In addition, she assists families in planning and making the transition from traditional school to online or homeschooling. Trained by Annemarie Roeper in qualitative assessment, Dr. Navan collaborates with families in understanding their gifted child's social-emotional qualities and needs.

In the area of professional development, Dr. Navan collaborates with school districts to provide teacher-centered services on methods of serving the gifted in the schools. She works with schools to design and deliver services districtwide, schoolwide, by subject or grade, or through individual coaching.

Dr. Navan has written numerous academic and community articles regarding the nature and needs of gifted individuals. She is the author of *Nurturing the Gifted Female: A Guide for Educators and Parents*. Her years of service include director of the Murray State Center for Gifted Studies, the Kentucky State Advisory Council for Gifted and Talented Education, the Kentucky Association for Gifted Education Board (KAGE), and the Board of Directors for Supporting Emotional Needs of Gifted (SENG). Dr. Navan is a member of the American Psychological Association (APA).

CPSIA information can be obtained
at www.ICGtesting.com
Printed in the USA
BVHW041257161021
618931BV00006B/186

9 781733 775823